Better Homes and Gardens®

Shade
Gardening Made Easy

Meredith Consumer Marketing
Des Moines, Iowa

Shade
Gardening Made Easy

MEREDITH CONSUMER MARKETING
Consumer Marketing Product Director: Heather Sorensen
Consumer Marketing Product Manager: Wendy Merical
Consumer Marketing Billing/Renewal Manager: Tami Beachem
Business Director: Ron Clingman
Senior Production Manager: Al Rodruck

WATERBURY PUBLICATIONS, INC.
Contributing Editor: Karen Weir-Jimerson, Studio G, Inc.
Contributing Copy Editor: Peg Smith
Contributing Proofreader: Carrie Truesdell
Contributing Indexer: Donald Glassman

Editorial Director: Lisa Kingsley
Creative Director: Ken Carlson
Associate Editors: Tricia Bergman, Mary Williams
Associate Design Director: Doug Samuelson
Production Assistant: Mindy Samuelson

BETTER HOMES AND GARDENS® MAGAZINE
Editor in Chief: Stephen Orr
Managing Editor: Gregory H. Kayko
Creative Director: Michael D. Belknap
Senior Associate Editor, Gardening: Jane Austin Miller

MEREDITH NATIONAL MEDIA GROUP
President: Tom Harty

MEREDITH CORPORATION
Chairman and Chief Executive Officer: Stephen M. Lacy

In Memoriam: E.T. Meredith III (1933–2003)

Pictured on the front cover:
top left 'White Lights' azalea is a spring-flowering shrub that is cold hardy to Zone 4.
bottom left Astilbe brightens shady gardens with feathery spires in pink, red, and white.
right A shaded woodland border can be a brilliant tapestry when planted with colorful perennials, shrubs, and trees.

Copyright © 2015
Meredith Corporation.
Des Moines, Iowa.
First Edition.
Printed in the United States of America.
ISBN: 978-0-696-30215-2

All of us at Meredith Consumer Marketing are dedicated to providing you with information and ideas to enhance your home. We welcome your comments and suggestions. Write to us at: Meredith Consumer Marketing, 1716 Locust St., Des Moines, IA 50309-3023.

Contents

Chapter 1

Chapter 2

Chapter 3

Chapter 4

76
GARDEN PLANS

Create the garden of your dreams with customized plans for shady areas.

Chapter 5

96
LIVING THE SHADY LIFE

Discover how creative homeowners turn shaded spots into lush and verdant landscapes.

Chapter 6

140
SHADE PLANTS ENCYCLOPEDIA

Uncover a world of colorful options for shaded landscapes using a variety of plants from small to tall.

CHAPTER ONE

Shade Gardening Basics

Transform dark spots in your landscape into islands of color and texture.

Gardening in the Shade

Color your landscape with a wide range of leafy and flowering shade-loving annuals, perennials, shrubs, and trees.

Shade often gets a bad rap with homeowners who feel planting choices are limited. But the same is true for homeowners who have no shade at all. There is a finite list of plants that can thrive in an all-sun garden. There is also a finite group of plants that grow in shade. And the lists of plants that flourish in shaded spots and those that worship the sun are totally different. That's because each plant—annual, perennial, shrub, and tree—has a specific preference for a specific type of light. Some like sunny locations, and others need shade to live happily. And there are some plants that thrive in areas that fall between sun and shade: spots that receive dappled light or sun for part of the day and shade for the other.

The opportunity of shade

When you look at shade as an opportunity, the world of gardening possibilities opens. Thanks to the adaptability of plants, many species grow well in low-light areas. Shade gardens can be lush and exquisite landscapes populated with an amazing variety of colors and textures. Gardeners have so many shade-loving options: small woodland wildflowers, spring-flowering bulbs, leafy perennials, colorful annuals, flowering shrubs, and understory trees. As a shade gardener, you'll find that you can enjoy a great number of leafy and flowering plants that will transform a dark, shaded area into a dreamy wonderland.

The seasons of shade

For those who want to garden in the shadow of trees or buildings, there is good news: A multitude of flowering and foliage options excel in sunless spots. In fact, gardeners with shaded areas in gardens and landscapes have a surprising number of planting options in a variety of plant types.

Like all gardens, shade gardens change appearance by season. Shade gardens can be colorful in all seasons by including plants that perform at their peak at different times. For example, spring brings a long-awaited flush of flowers from shade-loving perennials such as old-fashioned bleeding heart, Virginia bluebells, and spring-flowering bulbs. Summer shade gardens are adorned with leafy hostas, colorful heucheras, and astilbe with plumes of red, pink, and white. Late summer and fall shade gardens feature flowering beauties such as turtlehead, fall crocus, and tiarella.

Take a page from nature's playbook

A walk through woods, forest, or jungle reveals plants that have adapted to low-light growing conditions. They are naturals at living beautiful and leafy lives without direct sun. From woodland wildflowers that pop open on the forest floor in early spring to bright tropicals with colorful leaves and flowers, the plant world has adapted beautifully to producing plants that grow in semi-darkness. A bounty of small trees and shrubs excel in dark spots, requiring shade from larger trees to flourish. The natural beauty of woodlands, forests, and jungles can inform and educate gardeners about the lush, colorful, and ever-changing possibilities of shade gardens.

opposite, far left Hostas are the heroes of the shade garden, offering large leaves in a variety of colors: green, chartreuse, blue, and variegated. *opposite, top right* The intricate heart-shape flowers of old-fashioned bleeding heart appear in early spring. *opposite, middle right* Fern leaves rise from the ground and unfold with beautiful drama. *opposite, bottom right* Variegated hostas, whose green leaves are splashed with yellow and white, bring bright color to shaded spaces.

Gardening in the Shade

Trees and shade

The tree species in your yard provide differing shade. For example, large-leaf species, such as maple and sycamore, create deep shade on the ground below. Plants that grow in deep shade include ferns and hostas. Fine-leaf trees, such as honey locust and mountain ash, offer filtered light, and plants that like partial shade will thrive below them. Leafy trees offer different shade than conifers. A deciduous tree on the south side of a house will block summer sun, then when it sheds its leaves, it allows winter light to pass through. Evergreens shield light in all seasons.

Making shade

If you don't have shade in your yard, you can plant trees, shrubs, and tall perennials to create shaded areas for growing shade-loving plants. In addition, there are other landscape elements, such as buildings, trellises, sunshades, and umbrellas, that create areas for shade-loving plants to thrive.

You can also create shade by planting vines or tall annual flowers, such as sunflower. These plants can provide shade to an area within a single summer.

Although shrubs and trees aren't as fast growing, they provide shade to areas for the long term. To avoid constant pruning, select shrubs with the mature height and width you want, and set them far enough from walls, walks, patios, and property lines to allow space to grow and flourish. Most deciduous shrubs reach mature height within three growing seasons. Evergreens, such as arborvitae, take longer.

Trees, of course, take much longer to grow into shade-producing structures. Fast-growing species such as poplar, silver maple, and willow make quick shade but have short life spans. Adding slow-growing, long-lived trees, such as oaks and maples, is a good long-term landscaping strategy.

right Hosta and tiarella are beautiful shade garden partners.
opposite, top right The soft plumes of astilbe come in white, red, and pink. *opposite, bottom right* Combining plants with varying leaf textures creates beautiful partnerships. Round, flat hosta leaves provide contrast for lacy fern leaves.

Identifying Light in Your Yard

Light patterns change every couple hours. Determining overall light in your yard will help you choose the right plants.

Satisfy tree and shrub sunlight needs and you're well on your way to a thriving landscape. Many woody plants require bright sunlight, yet several grow and bloom in part shade or even full shade. Pairing a plant with its preferred light level begins with studying the sunlight that bathes the landscape.

Shade and sun

Ideally, gardens have some shade and some sun. To figure out the amount of shade and sun yours has, orient yourself to the north and other compass points of your yard. Then make notes of sunrise and sunset and the shadow on the different parts of the yard at varying times of day and year.

Once you have a good idea of year-round shade and sun patterns in your yard, devise a growing plan. If you have mostly shade due to existing trees, your planting plan may involve understory trees (those than can grow in the shade of larger trees) and shade-loving shrubs, perennials, and annuals.

Take inventory of sunlight

Assess light patterns every couple of hours during the course of a day, noting where shadows fall, linger, and pass. Where you see sunlight trails during spring, bare-branched trees are creating the illusion of sunny spots beneath. What looks like a sunny area may be swallowed by shade after leaves emerge. Buildings and walls also cast shadows; take those structures into account as you plot the sun's path.

As you assess light patterns, consider plant growth. A 15-foot-tall maple will cast a much greater shadow in five years than it does now. Base sunlight estimates on mature plant size.

opposite top Shade patterns change over the course of a season. The perennials near this deciduous tree receive ample sunlight in early spring before the tree leafs out. *opposite bottom* Plant perennials and bulbs, such as primula, forget-me-not, and narcissus (*left to right*), to add bright or soft color.

Once you have a general idea of how many hours of daily sunlight various areas throughout your yard receive, consider the best plants for those conditions. As you read about trees and shrubs, you'll encounter light requirements. Light needs are often expressed as full sun, part sun (partial sun), part shade (partial shade), or full shade. These terms refer to the amount of sunlight a plant needs to yield top-notch performance. Deciphering these labels can be confusing.

Full-sun plants require at least six hours of sun per day. The quality of the sunlight is important. A tree or shrub labeled as requiring full sun needs six hours of direct sunlight, not light filtered through a canopy.

Part-sun plants ideally receive three to six hours of direct sun per day, preferably in morning or evening, not during the hottest parts of the day. Part-shade plants will thrive with three to six hours of sun per day, but definitely require shade during the afternoon, when the sun is hottest. These conditions describe small trees and shrubs growing underneath mature trees where the sun slants during the morning. The east side of a building also offers part shade.

Full-shade plants need fewer than three hours of direct sun per day. Filtered sunlight or light shade is necessary for the rest of the day. This could describe plants on the north side of a structure or under a spreading tree where sunlight briefly penetrates the canopy at some point during the day and plants grow in light-filled shade the rest of the day.

Regional influences

Light requirements for trees and shrubs shift throughout the country. In the South and Southwest, shrubs that grow well in full sun in the North, such as many hydrangeas, need shade during the hottest part of the day. In the Pacific Northwest, cloud cover can prevent sun lovers from flourishing. Where cool, wet summers prevail, plants that prefer part shade can thrive in sunnier conditions.

Perennials and Annuals

Paint dark spaces with colorful and textural talents of shade-loving perennials and annuals.

Shade-loving perennials and annuals add dramatic color and texture in shade gardens. For the most diversity, use a combination of both types of plants. Perennials have the advantage of coming back each year, while annuals provide season-long color and intrigue. Together, they add interest from early spring through autumn.

Consider color

A shade garden will never be as colorful as a sun garden. But you can still enjoy beautiful blooms and flashy foliage from shade perennials and annuals. For example, colorful shade perennials include astilbes that bloom in pink and red, and lamium, Virginia bluebells, and vinca that produce blue flowers. A plant with the unfortunate name of lungwort (*Pulmonaria*) features silvery, lung-shape spots that dot the foliage. The variegated foliage holds all season long and is an especially nice accent to clusters of pink, white, or blue flowers that appear in spring.

Shade annuals include showy begonias in pink, red, and white as well as impatiens that bloom in a wide range of colors. Many white-flowering shade lovers, such as hosta and goatsbeard, as well as foliage plants are splashed with white that lightens shady areas.

Tap into texture

Foliage and flowering plants can create beautiful textural mosaics in a shade garden. For example, ferns offer finely cut foliage and thrive in some of the darkest areas of the garden. Ferns range in size from small to large and have many leaf patterns, variegated color, and fronds that unfurl. Some varieties of hosta feature leaves that range from sword-shape and slender to large, round, or puckered leaves.

Make creative combinations

Consider how plants look together when you add perennials and annuals to your shade garden. Choose and combine plants that are different from one another, creating a contrast that highlights the charms of both plants. For example, combine large-leaf plant varieties with narrow-leaf varieties to make a visual effect that shows off what is so beautiful about each plant.

Creative combinations may also be plants that bloom at the same time or in succession. For example, Virginia bluebells rise and bloom in early spring, then the plants go dormant (and all but disappear) when temperatures heat up. By pairing this beauty with other spring-blooming favorites, such as daffodils and bleeding heart, the combination is stunning from early to late spring.

Choreograph by season

Each shade perennial has a season in which it shines. When planting, think about adding color, texture, and visual interest for each season. Spring-blooming perennials include pulmonaria, hellebore, and primula. Summer-flowering shade perennials include astilbe, hosta, and goatsbeard. And fall-flowering shade perennials include turtlehead and aster. In addition, blooming bulbs that come back year after year add color to shaded areas. Spring-flowering bulbs include narcissus, tulip, and crocus. Summer-blooming bulbs include allium and various lilies. Even a fall-blooming crocus colors shaded landscapes in autumn.

Supplement with annuals

Shade-loving annuals look good from spring to fall, which is a great talent in the garden. By combining them with perennials, you ensure a colorful, active, and beautiful shade garden and landscape all season.

opposite left Astilbe grows in several types of light, from partial shade to sun; it's an ideal perennial for yards with varying light **opposite, top right** Ferns offer finely cut foliage and thrive in some of the darkest spots in the garden. **opposite, middle right** A mix of shrubs, perennials, and annuals fills dark spaces with bright color. Spotted laurel stands above hostas and impatiens. **opposite, bottom right** Caladium, a tropical bulb, has fascinating splashes of pink, white, and green.

Build a hosta-filled bed around the base of shade trees for a beautiful and low-maintenance garden.

Trees and Shrubs

Trees and shrubs usually provide shade for other plantings. Some varieties thrive in the shade of larger trees.

Trees are important in every landscape. Whether your yard is large or small, in an urban or rural setting, trees add structure, color, and texture to the surroundings. They also provide shade for plants that grow beneath them. Nearly every yard has room for small trees, and they add character to the landscape.

Large and small trees

Trees add structure to the landscape. While large trees are shade makers, there are many smaller tree species that grow well in the shade beneath. When buying a tree for your landscape, check the plant tag for the required light conditions; some trees need more light than others. Tree species that grow in light shade include red maple, Japanese maple, red buckeye, and European and American hornbeam. For heavily shaded areas, try serviceberry and pawpaw.

Shade-loving shrubs

Landscaping a shady backyard is easy when you choose from a select group of shrubs that excel in low-light situations. Some will even produce colorful and fragrant flowers. Shrubs play an important role in the shade landscape because they provide structure, form, and four-season interest. Good options include azalea, rhododendron, hydrangea, and mountain laurel. There are a few evergreen shrubs that excel in shade, including yew, cedar, and hemlock. Some varieties are more shade-tolerant than others, so check the plant tag for light requirements.

FLOWERING SHRUBS FOR SHADE

These shrubs bloom in part shade. Perfect for the north or east side of a home, they add color to the landscape for weeks.

1. OAKLEAF HYDRANGEA Large showy cone-shape flower clusters in summer; striking red, orange, and yellow fall color. Zones 5–9

2. CAMELLIA Flowers in shades of white, pink, or red bloom in fall, winter, and early spring; plants thrive in the shade of pines. Zones 7–11

3. SUMMERSWEET CLETHRA Fragrant white, pink, or rose flowers in midsummer; grows well in moist soil. Zones 4–9

4. WITCH HAZEL Boldly fragrant yellow or red flowers bloom for several weeks in late winter or early spring. Zones 5–8

5. BOTTLEBRUSH BUCKEYE White flowers are 8 to 12 inches long in early summer; spreading shrub grows 12 feet tall and wide. Zones 4–8

6. MOUNTAIN LAUREL Showy white to deep pink flowers in late spring or early summer. Evergreen foliage is a valuable asset. Zones 4–9

7. SPICEBUSH Green-yellow flowers in mid-spring; scarlet fruit ripens in late summer through October and attracts birds. Zones 4–9

8. FOTHERGILLA Cream-color bottlebrush-like flowers in spring; bold yellow, orange, and red fall color. Zones 5–8

Adding Color and Light

How do you brighten shaded gardens? Pick from a palette of blooming and variegated plants to shine light in the darkness.

Turn on the lights in gardens, especially along pathways, by adding colorful or variegated plants. Variegated is a term that refers to a lighter color on the leaves, such as white, yellow, or cream. Variegated varieties of plants, especially foliage plants, introduce light color into shade gardens.

The value of variegation

Variegation happens in plants naturally, as a condition of genetics. White edging (or variegation) in a hosta leaf, for example, happens because of a plant's inability to produce pigment in that area of the leaf. Darker colors of variegation (yellow, light green, or orange) are produced from a reduced production of green pigment. These genetic abnormalities are encouraged by plant breeders because variegation is so attractive in the garden.

Infusing white accents

Another way to add bright highlights in a shade garden is by planting drifts of white-flowering perennials. Perennials that sport white blooms include old-fashioned bleeding heart, hosta, bigroot geranium, astilbe, and trillium. Annuals with white flowers include begonia, calla lily, impatiens, and vinca. Spring-flowering bulbs (that grow in dappled shade beneath dormant deciduous trees) include scilla, crocus, allium, and daffodil.

opposite, left Add bright and colorful ornaments or artwork as a focal point in a shade garden. *opposite, top right* Variegated bishop's Weed (*Aegopodium podagraria* 'Variegata') is an easy-care groundcover. *opposite, middle right* White masterwort (*Astrania major*) is a shade-loving perennial. *opposite, bottom right* *Brunnera* 'Jack Frost' turns on the lights in shade.

COLORFUL SHADE PERENNIALS

Here's a sample of the bright bloomers available for shade gardens.

1. BIGROOT GERANIUM (*Geranium macrorrhizum*) One of the toughest plants that grow in the shade garden, bigroot geranium doesn't mind heat or drought. This shade plant puts on a spring show with pink or white flowers; some varieties also offer outstanding fall coloration in woodsy-scented foliage.

2. TOAD LILY (*Tricyrtis*) Put on a fall show with shade plant toad lily. This easy-to-grow perennial offers unique flowers that are often compared to orchids. Many are spotted with purple or blue.

3. AJUGA (*Ajuga* sp.) Also known as carpetweed or bugleweed, ajuga forms a 6-inch-tall mat of glossy leaves that look neat and fresh. Leaves are purple, white, silver, cream, or pink.

4. OLD-FASHIONED BLEEDING HEART (*Dicentra spectabilis*) There's little wonder why old-fashioned bleeding heart is a favorite that grows in shade. In late spring and early summer, it produces pink or white heart-shape flowers that hang from elegant, arching stems.

5. HOSTA (*Hosta* sp.) Hostas are among the showiest and easiest-to-grow perennials that prefer shade. They offer the most variety of any shade plant. Choose from miniatures that stay only a couple of inches wide or giants that sprawl 6 feet across or more. Look for leaves in hues of green, blue, white, chartreuse, and gold, with many variegated cultivars. Some hosta flowers are very fragrant.

CHAPTER TWO

Shade Garden Know-How

Plant selection, site preparation, and solid planting techniques ensure success.

Choosing Healthy Plants

Start with healthy plants to ensure garden success.

Plants with strong root systems and healthy leaves, stems, and trunks easily transition into new gardens. Because trees and shrubs command a sizable investment, it pays to shop smart and examine plants before making a purchase.

Where to shop

Perennials, trees, and shrubs are sold at garden centers and home centers and through mail-order and online companies. Garden centers likely have the largest selection of plants and the greatest diversity of species for specific areas. Often staffed with knowledgeable salespeople, garden centers are reliable places to ask questions about the best plants for your yard and seek planting advice appropriate for your Zone.

Try a home center or large retailer when you need a large number of uniform plants. The woody plant selection at a home center is slimmer than at a garden center, and plants may not be well-tended. Prices at home centers are often lower than those at garden centers. The best way to succeed with home center plants is to purchase them as soon as possible after they arrive at the store. Most home centers receive plants on particular days of the week; learn the delivery schedule and shop shortly thereafter.

What to look for

Search for quality rather than quantity when choosing woody plants. A small tree with a sturdy, straight trunk and well-positioned branches is a better long-term investment than a large tree with many wayward branches and a blemished trunk. Foliage color and shape as well as branching structure should be appropriate for the plant.

above Most garden centers and nurseries have separate sections for shade plants. Be sure to read plant tags carefully to ensure the plants you pick are suited to low-light environments.

Nurseries grow and sell trees and shrubs in containers and wrapped in fabric. Plastic containers are commonly used to raise woody plants. Field-grown trees and large shrubs are harvested then wrapped in burlap around the root balls and secured with nails, string, or wire. These plants are called balled-and-burlapped (B&B). The root balls contain field soil, as opposed to lightweight potting mix, so they are heavier to handle than container-grown plants. Because the roots are established in water-holding field soil, they will not dry out as quickly as plants grown in fast-draining potting soil.

Healthy roots

Inspect each plant's root system. A healthy root system helps trees and shrubs overcome transplanting stress and quickly establish in the landscape. Container-grown plants should be firmly rooted in the soil. Check the strength of the root system by pushing the tree trunk or shrub back and forth while holding the root ball still. The base of the tree or shrub should not move. Next, locate the top layer of the plant's roots; they should be within an inch or two of the soil surface. Sometimes plants are planted too deeply in containers. The raised soil level can hinder growth and even cause death, especially for trees.

Balled-and-burlapped trees and shrubs should have a solid root ball. A loose or droopy ball indicates the plant does not have a strong root system and might not grow well in the landscape.

Be wary of large plants

Bigger is not always better when buying trees and shrubs. Container-grown plants with a large amount of above-ground growth should have a sizeable root mass. If a 4-foot-tall shrub is squeezed into a 1-gallon pot, its root system is likely compromised, and transplanting into the landscape will stress the plant and slow its growth. When given a choice, opt for a smaller plant relative to the size of the root ball. When stems and leaves are somewhat proportional to the roots, the plant will establish rapidly in a new setting.

TREE AND SHRUB BUYING TIPS

HEALTHY ROOTS Check roots close to the base of the trunk. Look for kinked or circling roots near the soil surface. Both are signs of root problems. Don't buy the plant. Inspect the bottom of the container for escaping roots, which should be no larger than the diameter of a pencil. Next, lay the plant on its side and slip it out of the container. The root ball should stay together, and a few roots should be visible near the outer edge of soil. If many roots create a ring around the root ball, the plant is likely pot-bound. Choose a different plant.

STRONG TRUNK Strong trunks are thickest near the ground and taper as they rise. They do not need stakes for support. Test trunk strength by taking the tree to an open area and removing all stakes. If the tree is in leaf and remains erect, it is probably strong enough. The trunk should be free of scrapes and dents. Trunk damage at a young age is challenging to overcome and could compromise the health and strength of the tree as it ages.

APPROPRIATE BRANCHING Well-positioned branches are important on trees. Branches should be distributed along the trunk and not clumped toward the top. Look for a pleasing branch arrangement, inspecting all sides of the tree. Branching is also important on shrubs, but because shrubs have many branches and are typically shorter-lived than trees, branching is not as critical. Look for plants with a balanced appearance on all sides and strong, unblemished branches.

AVOID CIRCLING ROOTS

Before purchasing a plant, slip it out of its growing container. Look at the perimeter of the root ball. You should see several small, fine roots and maybe a few larger roots on the edge of the soil ball. Avoid plants that have masses of thick roots encircling the root ball. These plants have been in containers too long and are difficult to establish in the landscape.

Preparing a Planting Site

Site preparation makes planting easier. Removing sod and adding amendments give newly planted trees and shrubs an ideal start for growth.

Site preparation depends on the size of planting project. A single tree requires a few minutes of prep time, but a mixed shrub border can easily encompass a day's work. Whether the site demands five minutes or five hours of preparation for planting, don't skip this important step. An investment of time now will reward you with trees and shrubs that have years of strong, healthy growth.

Tree tips

If soil and light conditions in a planting site are good matches for the new tree, very little site preparation is required. Take time to thoroughly remove sod from the planting area with a sharp spade. Rogue grass will quickly regrow around the young tree's trunk. Grass close to the tree trunk increases the chance of trunk injury during mowing. Also remove any construction debris from the planting site. Lumber, chunks of concrete, shingles, and other debris have the potential to impede growth.

Prepare a shrub bed

Large planting beds are excellent sites for shrubs as well as trees. Mimicking plants grown in nature, planting beds create a mass of color and texture that blends well with the existing landscape. Large beds are a maintenance benefit, too. Instead of many small trees and shrubs to mow around, a planting bed is one contiguous shape that allows for fast and easy mowing. A thick blanket of mulch between young plants suppresses weeds. The new plants will quickly grow together, shading the soil and preventing weeds.

Removing existing vegetation and eliminating compaction are the primary goals when preparing a planting bed. Use a sharp spade or rent a sod cutter to skim away sod. Soil around newly built homes and high-traffic areas, such as near an entryway, is often compacted. Compacted soil has little space for oxygen to make its way to plant roots and is often poorly drained. Incorporate a 3-inch layer of well-decomposed compost

in the top 8 to 12 inches of soil to make the soil more porous and add valuable nutrients. If you have the opportunity, always incorporate compost prior to planting.

MAKE A PLANTING BED

Time and effort spent preparing a planting bed for shrubs is always a good investment. A sharp spade and well-decomposed compost are all you need, but a sod cutter and rototiller will make quick work of big projects. Prepare the planting bed when existing soil is moist but not wet—a handful of soil should form a clump that breaks apart easily when squeezed.

1 REMOVE SOD
Begin by skimming off sod. Use a sharp spade or rent a sod cutter from a home improvement center. Cut deep enough to remove the sod's entire root zone. Cutting about 2 inches below the crown of the plant is usually sufficient. Add the sod to your compost pile, where it will decompose to form rich compost.

2 ADD COMPOST
Blanket the planting bed with a 3-inch layer of compost. Well-decomposed compost is essential. The material should be black, soft, and sweet smelling. Compost that contains chunks of bark, leaves, and other brown debris is not fully decomposed and can limit nitrogen available to new plants.

3 MIX INTO SOIL
Incorporate compost into the top 8 to 12 inches of soil. Using a sharp spade, turn and mix the compost and soil together. Use a rototiller to quickly incorporate compost in a large planting bed.

opposite Remove sod and weeds in a planting area, then add amendments to the soil to help new plants gain a healthy root hold.

above When planting a container, add enough potting mix to place plants near the top of the container, keeping them at a depth comparable to nursery pots. **far left** Keep terra-cotta containers indoors during winter to keep them from breaking in cold weather. They will last for years with proper care. **left** When you discover plant roots tightly bound as you remove it from a nursery pot, gently squeeze the root ball to loosen it and tease loose roots before planting.

Planting in Containers

Attention to details ensures strong, healthy plants. Use these techniques and tips to make planting more satisfying.

Plant in place if the container will be too heavy to lift and move when filled.

Before planting in a terra-cotta or other porous pot, soak the pot in water. A dry clay pot absorbs moisture from soil, taking water away from plants.

Fill a container half to three-quarters full with potting mix. Blend in slow-release fertilizer and, if desired, water-retentive crystals. Top with plain potting mix.

Arrange plants while still in nursery pots. Set them in the container, largest or tallest first, then finish with smaller plants.

Place the largest plant in the center of the container for a symmetrical design, or off to one side for an asymmetrical display. Rearrange plants until you're pleased with the look.

Just before planting, dip each plant's root ball in a solution of water and root stimulator formulated for transplants (available where garden supplies are sold).

Remove one plant at a time from its nursery pot, starting with the largest. To dislodge a large plant from a nursery pot, gently lay the pot on its side and press firmly on it with your foot. Roll the pot to the opposite side and repeat the process. Then slide the plant out of the pot.

To plant, set the plant in the container and add potting mix around the root ball. Set smaller plants in place. Fill in between plants with soil mix, without packing the mix.

To plant seeds, sow them directly in a container filled with potting mix. Follow planting instructions on seed packets.

Leave 2 inches between the top of the soil mix and the rim of the container to allow for water and mulch.

After planting, moisten the potting mix thoroughly (until water runs out the pot's drainage hole).

THE DRAIN GAME

Every container must provide drainage, giving excess water an escape route.

SCREEN If a container's drainage hole is large, cover it with screening, newspaper, or a coffee filter to prevent soil from leaking out.

GRAVEL If a container has no drainage hole and you prefer not to drill one, create drainage space with a 2-inch layer of gravel.

LINER When lining a container with landscape fabric or plastic, cut drainage holes in the liner.

Planting Shrubs

In gardens, surrounding foundations, or as hedges, shrubs add structure, texture, and beauty.

The depth of the planting hole is critical to the success of a newly planted shrub. The top of the root ball should be even with the surrounding soil. If the soil is clay or poorly drained, position the root ball 2 inches above the soil line. As with trees, planting preparation for shrubs consists of digging a hole as deep as the root ball and two to three times as wide. Use existing soil as backfill, and tamp the soil lightly while backfilling to eliminate air pockets.

Space smart

When planting shrub borders, foundation plantings, and hedges, the space between shrubs is important. Planted too closely together, two shrubs will quickly overtake one another, and neither plant will develop a pleasing shape. Planting too closely also compromises plant health as shrubs compete for limited resources. Exceptionally generous spacing creates a polka-dot effect in the landscape, and relationships between plants are lost in expanses of open space.

To create a full, lush landscape in short order, arrange plants so the outer edge of their current forms are 2 to 3 feet apart. At this distance, the plants will grow together in a couple of years. Regular pruning will be necessary to maintain appearance. The trade-off is that the planting will look nearly mature from the time it is planted.

To limit maintenance and save dollars, place plants farther apart, using mature width as a guide. For example, if a viburnum has a mature width of 4 feet, plant another viburnum about 6 feet away.

left When planting balled-and-burlapped shrubs, pull the burlap away from the top of the root ball before backfilling the planting hole with soil.

Spacing near entryways, walkways, and windows is especially important. Plan at least a 1-foot buffer between shrubs and high-traffic areas or structures.

Plant spacing in a hedge depends on how quickly you would like the plants to grow together. Site plants closer together than their mature width, and the hedge will fill in more quickly. You'll also need more plants. Space the shrubs based on their mature width, and the hedge will take several years to fill in to create a screen, but the cost will be lower because you'll need fewer plants.

Good options for hedging shrubs that create a green wall of privacy in a shaded spot include upright yew, holly, and hemlock. To create a beautiful, informal flowering hedge, use viburnum, dogwood, rhododendron, or azalea.

PLANTING B&B

First remove all twine and wire around the trunk. Peel back the burlap to reveal the upper third of the root ball. If the root ball is circled by a wire basket, it can be left in place. Removing it can damage the root ball. However, use wire cutters to snip away portions of the basket that extend over the top of the root ball.

EASY WEED CONTROL

Weeds are not only unsightly, but they also absorb valuable moisture and nutrients. Control pesky weeds around newly planted trees and shrubs with these tips.

1. MULCH A 2- to 3-inch layer of mulch will suppress weeds. Spread around plants right after planting, mulch will prevent weeds for several months. Shredded wood, chopped leaves, pine straw, and cocoa hulls are all excellent mulch materials. As they break down, they add nutrients to the soil. Plan to top planting beds or the area around trees with a 1-inch layer of fresh mulch annually.

2. HERBICIDE Preemergent herbicides that prevent weed seeds from germinating need water for activation. Sprinkle preemergent herbicide granules on the soil around plants prior to rainfall. The herbicide must be reapplied throughout the season. Read the package labels for specific information. If trees or shrubs will benefit from additional nutrients, look for a preemergent herbicide that contains a slow-release fertilizer.

3. 10 MINUTES A WEEK Dedicate time to eradicating weeds at the base of trees and around shrubs. It's a cinch to pull weeds in simple foundation plantings and around three or four trees in just 10 minutes a week. Stay on top of weeding and plants will reward you with robust growth, plus the small weeds that emerge will be easy to pull.

Planting Trees

Adding a tree to your landscape or garden will provide future shade. And it's so easy.

Proper planting depth is the most important part of the tree-planting process. If you plant a tree at the right depth, it will have the ability to overcome a host of landscape challenges. If it is planted too shallow or too deep, growth is compromised, water and nutrients are not readily available, and the plant is more susceptible to a variety of pests.

Thankfully, root flares make it easy to plant at the correct depth. You'll notice the root flare at the base of every tree trunk. This is the slightly swollen area at the trunk base where the uppermost roots emerge. In most cases the root flare should be level with the surrounding soil.

Often trees are planted too deeply in the nursery and the root flare is covered with soil. At planting time, remove the excess soil across the top of the entire root ball to expose the root flare. When backfilling the tree, be sure to keep the area free of soil.

High and dry

If you plant in poorly drained soil or clay, set the tree so the root flare is about 2 inches above the surrounding grade. As roots emerge from the root ball, they will expand into soil near the surface, where water drains more freely and oxygen is more abundant.

HOW TO PLANT A TREE

There is an adage about the importance of a good planting hole. It goes something like this: It is better to put a 25-cent tree in a 2-dollar hole than a 2-dollar tree in a 25-cent hole. Take time to carefully dig an adequate-size planting hole, and the tree will be well on its way to a long life.

1 DIG HOLE
Using a sharp spade, dig a planting hole. The depth of the hole should be equal to the height of the root ball, never deeper. The planting hole should be two to three times wider than the root ball. Toss the excavated soil onto a piece of burlap or in a wheelbarrow to make planting and cleanup easy.

2 EXAMINE ROOTS
Carefully remove the tree from the pot. Examine the roots. If they circle the perimeter of the root ball, cut four equally spaced 1- to 2-inch-deep vertical slices into the root ball. The severed roots will stop circling and, over time, grow outward into the surrounding soil. Gently place the tree in the planting hole. For a balled-and-burlapped tree, gently roll the root ball into the planting hole. Remove any twine or portions of wire basket that could girdle the trunk.

3 CHECK DEPTH
The point where the roots flare out from the trunk should be even with or slightly above the surrounding grade. Ensure the tree is at the correct depth by placing a shovel handle across the hole. Using the handle as a guide, check planting depth. Always err on the side of planting a tree a little higher than the surrounding grade, especially if the soil drains slowly.

4 BACKFILL
Fill the planting hole about halfway with the excavated soil, breaking up clods and lightly tamping the soil to prevent air pockets. The handle end of a spade works well for tamping. Fill the hole the rest of the way and lightly tamp again. Build a 3-inch-tall berm around the edge of the planting hole, and spread a 2-inch layer of mulch over the soil surface. The berm and mulch will aid in water retention.

5 WATER
Finish planting by watering the tree well. Using a hose or watering can, gently drench the surrounding soil, delivering water slowly so as not to disturb the soil berm. The berm will corral water, preventing it from flowing away from the tree into the surrounding landscape.

opposite Serviceberries provide four-season color: flowers in spring, berries in summer, colorful leaves in fall, and interesting bark in winter.

left The soil around newly planted trees and shrubs dries out quickly. Plan to water young plants at least once a week. ***top*** A 2- to 3-inch layer of organic mulch benefits newly planted trees and shrubs; the most important is preventing soil moisture loss. ***above*** Protect the trunks of new trees from deer and rabbit damage by surrounding them with a length of drainage tile shortly after planting. The drainage tile can be left in place for several years as the trunk expands.

After-Planting Care

Keep trees and shrubs in top shape with the right care after they are planted. Water, mulch, and light pruning are easy tasks.

Caring for a new tree or shrub begins as soon as it is planted. As new woody plants receive timely, regular care for 8 to 12 weeks after planting, they establish a strong root system, increasing drought tolerance and the ability to mine nutrients. Give plants a strong start with these simple care tips.

Water deeply

The most important part of after-planting care is watering. Container-grown trees and shrubs are planted in fast-draining potting soil that dries out quickly in the landscape, especially in hot, windy conditions. Balled-and-burlapped plants are surrounded by field soil that retains water well, but they also require regular watering.

Differing soil conditions and weather patterns will affect the frequency and amount of water a plant needs. Check soil moisture by pushing your fingers into the soil 4 inches below the surface. If the soil is dry or just slightly moist at that depth, the plant needs water. It's important to note that overwatering causes just as much harm as underwatering. Be sure to check soil moisture in the root zone before watering.

A slow trickle of water from a garden hose or drip hose at the base of the plant is the best method to apply water. Slow watering ensures the entire root ball is moistened and promotes deep root growth.

Add a layer of mulch

Preserve soil moisture, suppress weeds, and add nutrients with organic mulch. Spread a 2- to 3-inch layer of mulch around a tree or shrub to form a 3- to 6-foot diameter covering around the plant. This wide mulch blanket will allow water to easily seep into the root zone. Keep mulch away from the tree trunk or shrub stems to prevent moist mulch from rotting the bark. Shredded wood, bark chips, pine needles, and cocoa hulls are good mulching materials.

No need to fertilize

Newly planted trees and shrubs do not need fertilizer. Excessive nutrients while plants are getting established in the landscape can lead to growth of excess leaves and stems that the limited root system cannot support.

After one growing season, pull away the mulch from around the plant and spread a 1-inch layer of well-rotted compost under the plant canopy. Replace the mulch. The compost will be pulled into the root zone by earthworms and soil insects, providing valuable nutrients to plant roots.

Pruning

Good news: Pruning is rarely needed after planting. Reputable nurseries prune plants prior to sale. At planting, the tree or shrub should be free of limbs that rub against each other, broken branches, narrow-angle branches, and co-dominant leaders. If a new plant is affected by any of these troubles, prune it to correct the problem.

BHG TEST GARDEN TIP

RARELY STAKE

Most container-grown and balled-and-burlapped trees do not need staking. Poor, shallow soils or excessively moist conditions at planting time call for short-term staking. If a tree must be staked, position the stakes as low as possible. Materials used to tie the tree to the stake should be flexible to allow the trunk to move slightly. Remove all staking material within a few months.

Spring

Summer

Fall

Winter

34

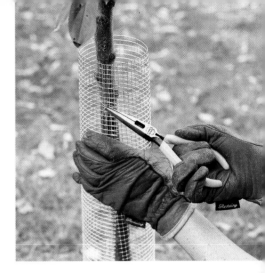

Seasonal Care

Trees and shrubs require minimal care to produce cooling shade, attractive flowers, and intriguing structure in the landscape. Use this quick checklist to keep your easy-care plants in top form.

Spring

Renew mulch Organic mulch slowly decomposes. Refresh the mulch around trees and shrubs by topdressing with a new thin layer of shredded bark, cocoa hulls, or other mulch. For optimum soil improvement and weed suppression, blanket the entire area under the drip line of trees and create a circle that extends about 1 foot beyond the outer branches of shrubs. Keep mulch away from the base of plants. Excess mulch near the base has the same effect as planting the tree or shrub too deeply.

Spread preemergent herbicide If you decide to use a weed killer, spread preemergent herbicide granules over shrub beds as soon as shrubs begin to leaf out. Be sure to follow package directions. Preemergent herbicide prevents weed seed germination for several weeks. It does not affect weeds that have already taken root; be sure to pull established weeds by hand.

Remove winter damage As trees and shrubs leaf out in spring, prune stems and branches that were damaged during winter. Candidates for pruning include branches broken from ice and snow as well as those killed by cold temperatures.

Plant early in season Take advantage of seasonal rains and cool soil temperatures, which promote root growth.

Summer

Combat drought Established trees and shrubs tolerate drought with ease. Plants will slow their growth to wait out the dry season. Young plants—those that have been on the site less than two years—benefit from supplemental watering during drought. To thoroughly soak the root ball, water with a drip hose or a slow trickle from a garden hose.

Prune Summer is time to prune most spring-blooming shrubs. Shortly after shrubs finish flowering, prune off excessive growth, crossing branches, and dead or diseased wood.

Fall

Wrap trunks of young trees Young, thin-barked trees, such as maples, are especially prone to sunscald. Similar to sunburn, sunscald is caused by bark heating by winter sun during cold weather and rapid refreezing, causing ice crystals to develop. It results in sunken, dried, or cracked bark. Prevent sunscald by wrapping trunks of young maple and honey locust trees with commercial tree wrapping, from the base of the trunk up to the first branch. Commercial tree wrap is available at many garden centers.

Prevent animal damage In winter, hungry mice and rabbits gnaw through bark, girdling stems. Deer eat stems and evergreen foliage as well as rub their antlers on young plants, causing extensive damage. Wrap or fence trees and shrubs to keep them from being eaten.

Plant new trees and shrubs Several months of cool soil temperatures and occasional rainfall make fall an ideal time to plant. Water new plants thoroughly, because they continue growing in early winter.

Winter

Prune Late winter is optimal to prune many trees and some shrubs. Leafless branches make plant structure easy to assess.

Consider repellents Commercial spray repellents are an effective means of protecting a large number of trees and shrubs from deer and rodents in winter. The repellents must be reapplied periodically. See package directions for details.

Spring Magnolias and other spring-blooming trees are candidates for pruning in early summer after flowers fade. **Summer** Variegated hydrangeas debut long-lasting flowers in early summer. **Fall** 'Pink Champagne' smoke tree lights up the fall landscape as soon as temperatures drop. **Winter** Trees and shrubs with long-lasting fruit add decorative elements to winter landscapes and important food sources for wildlife. **right** In fall, wrap vulnerable tree trunks with wire mesh or drainage tile to prevent damage caused by deer, rabbits, and mice.

above Hand-watering with an adjustable watering wand attached to a garden hose controls water flow with less waste and directs water into the soil. **far left** Water containers in early morning so leaves can dry off during the day; this will help prevent mildew. **left** Water-holding polymer crystals absorb moisture and dissolved nutrients, then gradually deliver them to plant roots as needed. Add crystals to potting mix before planting.

Watering

Consistent, routine watering is vital to plant health, especially for confined roots.

Containers usually require daily watering during summer or every two or three days during cool periods, unless nature handles it for you. Hot, dry weather and small pots can necessitate twice-daily watering.

Plants suffer from too much water as much as from too little. Determine whether a container garden needs water by poking a finger into the soil up to the second knuckle. If the soil feels dry, it's time to water. Check pots daily.

Saturate the potting mix thoroughly. Excess water should drain away from the containers. Soil sours, roots rot, and root-killing mineral salts build up in containers that drain poorly.

If a soilless mix dries out completely, rewet it by standing the pot in a large vessel of water for several hours.

Watering early in the day allows plants to soak up what they need before afternoon heat causes evaporation. Watering in the evening can leave moisture on foliage and promote disease.

Use a watering can to water a group of pots all at once.

Using drip irrigation set on a timer takes the work out of watering. A drip system also saves water by delivering water near plant root zones with as little evaporation and runoff as possible. Check the system seasonally, especially in hard-water areas, to make sure the timer works and lines are not clogged or punctured.

Self-watering pots feature built-in reservoirs that deliver moisture to soil and require less frequent watering. Water-holding mats fit into the bottom of hanging baskets and other containers, wicking moisture into the soil.

IRRIGATION MADE EASY

A simple-to-install drip irrigation system can be customized to suit your garden and to target your thirstiest plants.

DRIP IRRIGATION A drip system supplies water to containers via tubes branching from a main line. Use drip systems in garden beds, borders, and landscaping, or in containers.

SPRAY EMITTER Ideal for watering containers, place one emitter—attached to flexible tubing—in each container to supply water when needed. These irrigation systems can even be used in hanging baskets or window boxes.

AUTOMATIC TIMER An automatic timer turns a drip irrigation system on and off, handling the job for you. Timers make watering easy and are especially helpful for homeowners who travel often.

Fertilizing

High-performance plants need nutrients to produce vigorous foliage and bright blooms.

Annuals and perennials need fuel to produce flowers and foliage. Here are feeding tips:

Gradual-release plant food, blended into a potting mix before planting, offers an easy way to feed container plants continuously. Coated granules release nutrients slowly, usually over three to nine months, depending on the product.

If you use a standard potting mix that does not already include fertilizer, add gradual-release fertilizer according to package directions. Additional granules can be scratched into the soil mix later as a nutritional boost when needed.

Water-soluble plant food is an alternative. Make a solution of plant food and water, sprinkle it on the soil, and reapply it regularly throughout the growing season.

Plant food labels indicate—in a series of numbers separated by dashes—the balance of the major nutrients it supplies: nitrogen-phosphorus-potassium. An all-purpose, 14-14-14 fertilizer gives plants the primary nutrients they need to thrive.

Some plants need feeding more often, including those in close quarters or growing in a soilless mix. Fast-growing, vigorous plants benefit from regular feeding.

Edible plants and long-term plantings benefit from organic fertilizers that enrich soil and improve its structure. Organic fertilizers include compost, rotted manure, fish emulsion, and kelp products.

Plants show signs of nutrient deficiency particularly in foliage, alerting you to the need for fertilizer. Clues include pale or discolored leaves, weak or slow growth, and smaller leaves and flowers.

Taper off feeding as gardening season comes to its close.

SLOW AND STEADY
An easy way to feed plants, slow-release fertilizer supplies nutrients over a period of time. Check package directions for correct fertilizer amounts. With fertilizer, more is not better. In fact, too much fertilizer can harm plants.

left Sprinkle granulated fertilizer into potting mix before planting. **top** Scratch granular fertilizer into garden soil at the base of plants. **above** Give plants a boost at planting time with a water-soluble transplant fertilizer.

Mulching

Mulch is a funny word, but the stuff has a serious job. Mulching is not necessary, but it benefits gardens and keeps plants healthy.

Mulch prevents soil from washing out of pots and splashing onto to foliage when plants are watered.

Mulch insulates soil and plant roots, keeping them cool during hot summer days.

Organic mulches, such as cocoa shells and chipped or shredded bark, decompose gradually and add nutrients to the soil mix. Ornamental mulches, including pebbles, shells, and recycled glass, are pretty and effective materials.

Mulch deters squirrels, slugs, and other critters from pestering container plantings. Squirrels won't bother digging in gravel or medium- to large-bark mulch. Slugs avoid any gritty mulch.

How to mulch

In spring, after rain or watering, top the soil with a 1- to 2-inch layer of mulch. Apply it loosely and evenly; avoid compacting mulch and piling it up around plant stems.

Take advantage of the ornamental value of many mulches. Crushed recycled glass, polished river stones, marbles, and flat glass drops are available in a multitude of colors. They glisten when wet and reflect sunlight. Terra-cotta spheres and seashells are especially eye-catching.

Mix and match plants and mulches to find the most effective and pleasing combinations. For example, organic nutshells and fragrant cocoa shells work especially well in edible gardens; herbs and alpines have a proclivity for fine gravel.

opposite left Pine straw is an attractive mulch for shade gardens. **opposite, top right** A layer of amber recycled glass is a beautiful soil topper for a single succulent in a pot. **opposite, middle right** Cocoa shells are a beautiful fine mulch for small plants such as coleus or herbs. They have another attraction: the aroma of chocolate. **opposite, bottom right** Terra-cotta spheres look beautiful while protecting soil moisture. **right** Add shredded bark at the base of plants to help suppress weeds and control soil moisture.

Grooming

In just a few minutes a day, keep containers, beds, and borders healthy and vigorous. Combining grooming and watering in a routine provides an opportunity to spot disease or pest problems early.

A little nipping and tucking in your garden will help it look good as well as keep you aware of anything that can cause problems. A daily walk through your garden will allow you to do some quick cleanup and watch for evidence of pests, such as chewed leaves from deer or insect pests. These simple activities will keep your plants happy and healthy.

Deadheading

Remove flowers as soon as they begin to shrivel, fade, or otherwise appear spent. Snip them off with your fingers or use pruners.

Pinching off spent flowers also helps prevent annuals from completing their life cycle and producing seeds, which promotes longer blooming.

While you're at it, remove any discolored or damaged foliage. Snip off and compost; or if it looks like the foliage is diseased, destroy it rather than composting.

Pruning

Snip back fast-growing or untidy plants that show signs of unruliness or unattractive bare stems.

Trim a plant for better shape in graceful proportion to the container or planting companions. Cutting off foliage reinvigorates the plant and helps produce more growth.

Prevent annuals from becoming scraggly or overgrown by midsummer, trimming 1 to 2 inches from them every other week. If plants become scraggly and bloom less, cut them back by one-third to one-half. Then fertilize the plants and watch them rebound quickly.

Replanting

By late summer or early fall, when some plants have passed their peak and appear bedraggled, it is time to replace them. Use a hand trowel to carefully lift a declining plant from its container and replace it with a new one. For example, when cool-weather annuals wilt in summer heat, replace them with heat-loving varieties.

Long-term plantings need rejuvenating, too. After two or three years, remove the tree, shrub, or perennial from the pot. Trim as much as one-third of the larger roots, especially those circling the root ball or tangled in tight masses. Loosen the root ball. Replant in a pot at least 2 inches larger with fresh potting mix.

Pests and diseases

Look for signs and symptoms of pests or diseases, such as disfigured or discolored foliage or visible insect pests. Take action right away.

Diagnose the problem accurately before taking steps to remedy it. Ask your local extension agent for help diagnosing the problem.

Treat the problem with the correct remedy. For example, not all insects are destructive in the garden. Treat only for those insects that are causing damage.

Handpick pest insects and drop them into a cup of soapy water. Or blast them off leaves with forceful spray from a garden hose. Remove and discard affected plant parts.

left Cut back perennials, such as soapwort, after plants bloom to encourage reblooming. *top* Look for plant munchers, such as slugs and snails, and remove them. *above* Deadheading entails cutting or pinching off flowers that have finished blooming.

CHAPTER THREE

Shade-Loving Containers

Easy-care pots of flowers and foliage are colorful additions to shade gardens.

Temporary Tenants

A jazzy arrangement of striking foliage plants in a wooden crate brightens any shady spot. Consider houseplants when stocking your container garden. You'll find dozens of selections with colorful foliage and tropical texture to round out your displays.

Essentials

Container: 14×22×10-inch salvaged wooden crate

Light: Shade

Water: Keep soil moist

Plant List

A. 1 caladium

B. 1 schefflera

C. 1 polka-dot plant

D. 1 Persian shield

E. 2 variegated ivy

Eye on the Prize

Highlight a container garden by placing it at eye level, where it will attract attention. An overturned crate or a substantial pot stands in as a stylish pedestal.

Know-How Notes

The built-in handles of this sturdy crate make it easy to tote. All plants can remain in individual containers. Gradually expose them to new digs with bright natural sunlight to avoid burning the leaves. Move plants back indoors before chilly weather returns in fall.

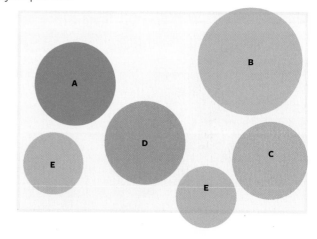

Shining in Shade

Plantings that show off a bonanza of bright colors and interesting or contrasting textures stand out in shade. Gleaming metallic containers reflect light, becoming veritable beacons that stand out among the plants.

Essentials

Container: 10-, 12-, and 16-inch galvanized metal pots

Light: Shade

Water: Keep soil moist

Plant List

Pot 1

A. 1 perilla ('Gage's Shadow')

B. 1 caladium ('Florida Elise')

C. 1 purple-leaf heuchera

Pot 2

D. 1 New Guinea impatiens ('Sonic Cherry')

E. 1 oxalis ('Zinfandel')

Pot 3

F. 1 ponytail fern (*Asparagus densiflorus* 'Myers')

Know-How Notes

A triangular grouping of containers often ensures display success. Use the largest container as the apex or anchor of the group. Cluster the rest of the containers around it and off-center, contrasting them by height or width to strike a balance.

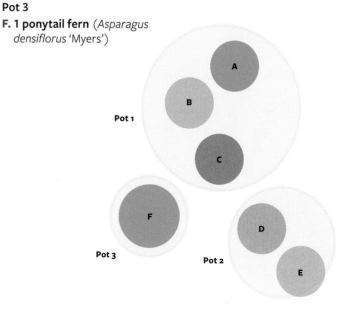

Square Root of Two

Let's face it: Containers can be expensive. These two, however, cost less than $20 to make yet are as stylish as pots costing fives times that amount. Assembling them takes little time and few materials.

Essentials

Materials to Make 2 Containers: Six 12×12-inch pavers, five 8×16-inch pavers, two 8×8-inch pavers, landscape block adhesive, caulking gun

Light: Shade

Water: Keep soil moist

Plant List

Planter 1

A. 1 elephant's ear ('Black Magic')

B. 1 alocasia

Planter 2

C. 2 coleus ('Inky Fingers')

D. 1 chartreuse hosta

E. 1 oshima sedge ('Evergold')

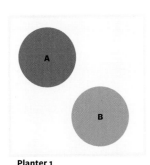

Planter 1

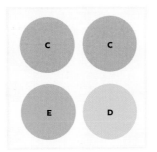

Planter 2

Know-How Notes

When attaching the bottom of the planter, use drops of adhesive rather than a solid bead to allow for channels through which water can drain.

Space Maker

Put together at least two planters. Using similar elements throughout a landscape creates coherence that's easy on the eyes and helps the elements— in this case, the planters— integrate into the setting. Also, a small space gains a sense of greater dimension with two or more planters of contrasting sizes.

MAKE A MODERN CONTAINER

Get a contemporary look with pavers and adhesive.

1 FORM THE SIDES
Stand four pavers on edge to make a square. Tilt one paver back and apply a bead of adhesive along the left and right inside edges. Press the paver against its neighbors to secure. Repeat on the opposite paver. Adjust the pavers to form a true square.

2 ATTACH THE BOTTOM
Apply drops of adhesive to the exposed edges of the pavers. Set the remaining paver on top; make sure all sides are straight.

3 SET THE PLANTERS IN PLACE
Allow 24 hours before moving the planters to your garden. Take care, though—the glue is fully cured in five to seven days. To raise planters off the ground, set them on the remaining pavers.

Over the Fence

Containers set on hard surfaces provide greenery, blooms, and a backdrop. Count on vines to grow up and adorn an adjacent fence. Add color at the base of the climbing plant using annuals and variegated ivy.

Essentials

Container: 28×10×10-inch fiberglass planter

Materials: 2×6-foot copper trellis

Light: Part shade

Water: Keep soil moist

Plant List

A. 1 clock vine (*Thunbergia grandiflora*)

B. 3 variegated English ivy

C. 2 yellow viola

Know-How Notes

A trellis gives vines a boost, supporting them as they grow. This vigorous vine clambers up and over the fence, decorating both sides.

Alternative Plantings

Employ pairs of fast-growing vines for a more colorful and dramatic focal point, such as black-eyed susan vine with nasturtium, or jasmine with creeping gloxinia (*Lophospermum erubescens*, aka *Asarina scandens*).

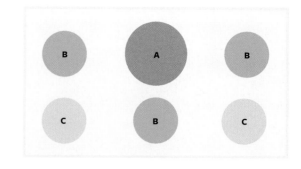

Ivy League

With portable planters you can grow plants almost anywhere. In this setting, movable containers create privacy on a patio. To form a wall, set two or more planters close together.

Essentials

Container: 36×12×12-inch cedar planter boxes

Materials: Two 7-foot rebar rods, 36-inch-wide wire rabbit fencing, wire, staked candleholders

Light: Part shade to shade

Water: Keep soil moist

Plant List

A. 8 English ivy

B. 2 yellow gazania

C. 2 red multiflora petunia

Know-How Notes

Stand the rods upright on opposite ends of the planter. Stretch the fencing taut between the uprights, securing it to them with twists of wire. Add staked candleholders to the planter for a finishing touch.

Ivy Varieties

If you don't find a pleasing variety of ivy at a garden center or nursery, look for it at a florists shop or where houseplants are sold.

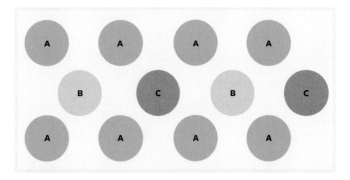

Yellow and Mellow

Monochromatic schemes make it easy to choose plants. This collection of plants that thrive in light shade feature yellow flowers and yellow-variegated foliage in a tub of sunshine on wheels.

Essentials

Container: 18-inch redwood or cedar planter

Materials: Three 4-foot-tall garden stakes; finial, if desired; dolly

Light: Part shade

Water: Keep soil moist

Plant List

A. 3 black-eyed susan vine

B. 1 variegated flowering maple

C. 2 heliopsis ('Loraine Sunshine')

D. 2 trailing vinca ('Illumination')

E. 1 lantana ('Samantha')

F. 2 variegated potato vine (*Solanum jasminoides*)

G. 1 coleus

Know-How Notes

Setting the planter on a sturdy dolly makes it easy to move into more or less sunlight. Secure the stake tops using a cap or wire. Plant a vine at the base of each stake.

Terrific Trellises

When you add a climbing or vining plant to a container garden, train the plant vertically to gain visual impact.

GROW UP

Here are easy options for structures for vines.

1 LEAN ON A PAINTED TRELLIS

A fragrant Madagascar jasmine gets plenty of support from a painted trellis leaning against the wall behind the potted plant.

2 SALVAGE A SUPPORT FROM NATURE

This variegated morning glory vine puts on a dramatic show all by itself. Given a windfall branch for support, the vine reaches high for the sky.

3 USE TIES TO HOLD UP VINES

Bamboo stakes capped with small terra-cotta pots make neat trellises for tomato plants in 18-inch pots. Tie the vines to the stakes to secure them.

SHADE-LOVING PERENNIAL VINES

Several hardy perennial vines will grow in shaded or partially shaded locations.

Boston ivy A vine that really shines in autumn for its fall color, Boston ivy bears three-lobe leaves that turn fiery red toward the end of the season. A relative of the grape, it bears clusters of small purple fruits that attract birds.

Dutchman's pipe An underused vine native to North America that deserves a lot more attention, Dutchman's pipe bears heart-shape leaves that can be up to 10 inches wide. It has unique flowers in spring, though they're often hidden among the beautiful foliage. This vine grows well in both sun and shade.

Climbing hydrangea The most elegant vine for shade, climbing hydrangea bears flattened clusters of fluffy white flowers in summer. Though the foliage may change to shades of yellow in the fall, it's not a reliable choice for producing autumn color in the garden. However, it is a sure pick for beautifying a shady wall or large fence.

Virginia creeper This vigorous vine bears dark green hand-shape leaves that turn bright red in fall. It can climb to 50 feet and is native to areas of North America.

Making an Entrance

Plants enhance any entryway with lively, continuous color. Raising plantings close to eye level makes them all the more welcoming (and able to receive light in this setting).

Essentials

Container: 14-inch footed cast-iron planter, 20-inch cast-iron planter on pedestal

Light: Shade

Water: Keep soil moist

Plant List

Pot 1

A. 1 maidenhair fern

B. 2 pansy

Pot 2

C. 1 maidenhair fern

D. 3 pansy

E. 2 English ivy

F. 1 hosta

Know-How Notes

Select containers that echo one another's color or shape for one of the easiest and most pleasing designs possible. Repeat some of the plantings to reinforce the effect.

Alternative Plantings

For colorful plantings in shade, try double impatiens (bright, plump flowers), caladium (showy foliage), and fuchsia (dangling flowers).

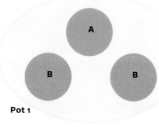

Pot 1

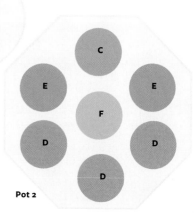

Pot 2

Facing North

Visible from indoors, a bright and colorful container brings cheer to the shady side of a house. The copper box and steel frame are made to last and sized to fit a standard window frame.

Essentials

Container: 36-inch steel window box frame with copper liner

Light: Shade

Water: Keep soil moist

Plant List

A. 4 impatiens 'Accent Pink Picotee'

B. 2 hosta 'Golden Tiara'

C. 2 Jacob's Ladder (*Polemonium* 'Brise d'Anjou')

D. 2 fuchsia 'Thalia'

E. 2 ground ivy (*Glechoma hederacea* 'Variegata')

F. 1 sweet potato vine (*Ipomoea batatas* 'Sweet Caroline Bronze')

G. 3 plectranthus 'Zulu'

Know-How Notes

Choose a window box at least 8 inches deep to give plant roots room to grow and to save you from watering more than once a day during hot weather.

Proper Mounting

Prevent future problems and damage to your house by properly mounting a window box. Using sturdy brackets or lag bolts (and lead anchors in a brick house), secure the box to the wall rather than the window trim.

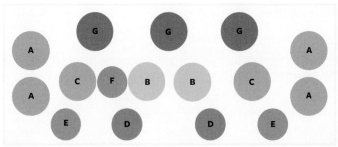

Step Right Up

Achieve fast, high-impact color in compact spaces—such as steps at an entry or a small deck—by grouping pots. Keep plantings simple with one to three varieties in each pot.

Essentials

Container: Six 12- to 16-inch glazed ceramic pots

Light: Sun to part shade

Water: When soil begins to feel dry

Plant List

A. 2 croton

B. 3 sweet potato vine

C. 1 hosta ('Sum and Substance')

D. 2 lantana

E. 5 pink vinca

F. 2 dusty miller

G. 1 sedum ('Autumn Joy')

Little Echoes

After you fill the nooks and crannies of flowerbeds with favorite annuals, tuck leftover plants into pots that will coordinate with the garden.

Know-How Notes

This garden in containers succeeds in part because the plant selection focuses on the entire composition rather than on individual pots. Repetition of chartreuse and pink tie the container plantings together in a pleasing combination of bold foliage and bright blooms.

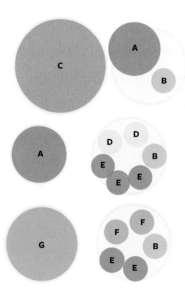

Little Landscape

To take advantage of vertical space, combine a small character-rich tree, such as dwarf Japanese maple, with an understory of plants in a large pot. Choose a tree variety that is hardy in your region.

Essentials

Container: 24×50-inch glazed pot

Light: Shade

Water: When soil begins to feel dry

Plant List

A. 1 dwarf Japanese maple

B. 1 toad lily (*Tricyrtis hirta*)

C. 1 moneywort ('Goldilocks')

D. 1 mondograss
(*Ophiopogon*)

Know-How Notes

This slow-growing tree and perennial companions are selected for foliage texture and color through the seasons.

Trees, Please

To add instant height to a potted garden with a dwarf tree or shrub, start with a young plant and allow plenty of room for its roots to grow inside the container. Eventually the tree or shrub will outgrow the pot and need to be transplanted into the landscape.

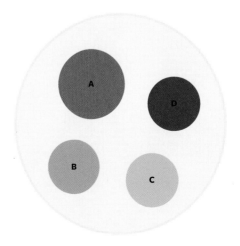

Home Sweet Home

These low-maintenance gardens feature easy-care plants with moderate growth rates, few pest or disease problems, and little upkeep besides watering. The all-foliage compositions boast bright hues and contrasting textures. A seasonal prop adds an element of fun.

Essentials

Container: Two 15-inch terra-cotta pots
Light: Part shade
Water: When soil feels dry

Plant List

Pot 1

A. 1 eastern hemlock

B. 1 heuchera ('Dolce Crème Brûlée')

C. 1 moneywort ('Aurea')

Pot 2

D. 1 sedum ('Angelina')

E. 1 blue fescue ('Elijah Blue')

F. 1 oregano ('Kent Beauty')

G. 1 juniper ('Holger')

Know-How Notes

Cold-hardy perennials rally around young conifers, enlivening the dragonscale planters continuously for a year or two in mild regions. Unless frostproof, in frigid climates pots should be emptied and stored and the plants given permanent places in the garden.

Labels are Telling

If the plant label doesn't specify a hardiness-zone range, you cannot be sure of the plant's viability in your region. Think twice about the purchase, unless you know the plant or intend to grow it as an annual.

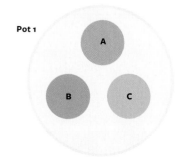

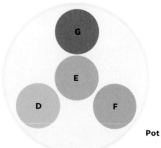

Evergreen Grace

Guided by a stout stake, this topiary's artful form takes advantage of naturally pendent branchlets. The evergreen companions highlight and echo it with silvery and blue-gray foliage, while the container makes its own strong statement.

Essentials

Container: 22-inch fiberglass planter

Light: Part shade

Water: When soil begins to feel dry

Plant List

A. 1 weeping blue atlas cedar ('Glauca Pendula')

B. 3 kale

C. 2 licorice plant

D. 2 blue flax

E. 1 blue fescue ('Elijah Blue')

F. 1 dusty miller

Know-How Notes

When a tree has been trained to exhibit an unusual form, it will likely come from the nursery attached to a sturdy stake. Leave the tree secured to this stake when transplanting the works into a new container. If the stake is flimsy, carefully replace it and secure the tree to a new support using soft ties.

Looking Good Year-Round

When you look for plants that will live contentedly in a container year-round, include a slow-growing tree or shrub. Possibilities include dwarf (meaning slow-growing or smaller than full-size species when mature) cultivars of evergreens, such as balsam fir, false cypress, juniper, mugo pine, and spruce.

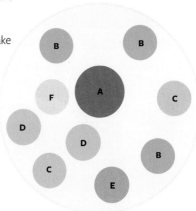

Twisted and Stout

This evergreen topiary adds personality to a lightly shaded garden. Shape a spiral-form juniper for a fraction of what ready-made ones cost at garden centers. Or start with a precut spiral and trim as needed.

Essentials

Container: 20-inch fiberglass pot

Light: Part shade

Water: When soil feels dry

Plant List

A. 1 upright dwarf juniper ('Hetz')

Super Swirlers

Dwarf Alberta spruce and boxwood are also good candidates for spiral-shape topiaries.

Know-How Notes

Start with a large (5- to 6-foot-tall) tree that's destined to reach a mature height of 15 feet unless you continually prune its central leader (main stem or trunk). Younger—smaller—trees cost less but will take more years to reach maturity.

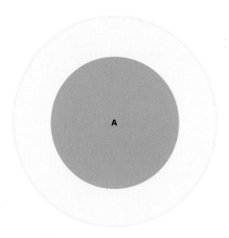

TRIM A TOPIARY

Try your hand at creating your own topiary. Snip, clip, and enjoy!

1 START AT THE BOTTOM

Use masking tape to mark areas to remain unclipped; plan to cut areas between the tape. Use sharp pruners to begin clipping the tree, working from the middle down and then up. Proceed slowly. Step back often and walk around the tree to view it from all sides.

2 AVOID CUTTING AGGRESSIVELY

Cutting close to bare wood removes greenery permanently; cutting near the branch tips encourages bushiness over time. Rough out the spiral, then remove the tape and refine the remaining greenery, shaping it into a rounded form using shears. The tree will look crude at first.

3 PREPARE FOR WINTER

In Zones 7 and warmer, the tree can grow in a pot year-round. In colder regions, transplant the tree to the garden in early fall. Or move the potted tree to a protected place over winter.

Leaps and Bounds

Compatibility with house color is key when placing a potted garden near a front door and wall. A vintage urn filled with bright tropicals and perennials complements the gold exterior color here.

Essentials

Container: 20-inch cast-iron urn

Light: Part shade

Water: When soil feels dry; pour water into the vaselike center of bromeliads

Plant List

A. 1 New Zealand flax
(Rainbow hybrid)

B. 1 lotus vine

C. 1 bromeliad

D. 1 croton

Know-How Notes

This garden is a natural in Zones 9–11, where these plants live outdoors year-round. It would be equally spectacular indoors.

Rule of Thirds

Let an accent or focal plant reach high and claim one-third of the design. Let one plant balance the effect as a low element, while supporting players fill out the design's other one-third.

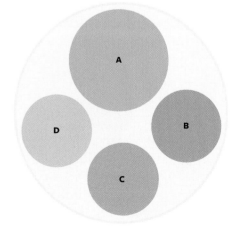

Rising Stars

This dramatic design has a practical side: It softens the transition from an expanse of yard to the hard upright surfaces of walls. The large, hefty pot holds a trellis for the climbing plants and enables the striking display, even in a small area.

Essentials

Container: 24-inch glazed ceramic pot

Light: Part shade to sun

Water: When soil feels dry

Plant List

A. 1 giant Burmese honeysuckle

B. 1 bacopa

C. 1 Santa Barbara daisy

D. 1 lilac vine (*Hardenbergia violacea* 'Happy Wanderer')

Alternative Plantings

Woody vines for cold climates include climbing hydrangea, porcelain berry (*Ampelopsis*), trumpet creeper (*Campsis radicans*), and wisteria.

Know-How Notes

Growing a woody vine in a container garden requires strong support. The trellis used in this scheme is anchored in the container then to the house. The vines can take annual pruning to rein in robust growth. Standing the container next to a porch pillar, balcony railing, or fence gives less-vigorous vines a leg up.

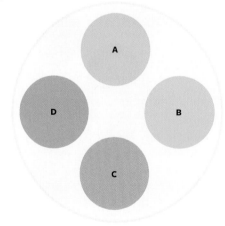

Water World

Assemble an attractive miniature aquascape in an afternoon. First choose a watertight container (one with dark interior minimizes algae growth). Then select from many kinds of water plants—some float, others just like to have wet feet.

Essentials

Container: 30×12-inch watertight ceramic bowl

Materials: Pea gravel, pump-filter-fountain unit, small rocks or broken bricks

Light: Part shade

Water: At least 2 inches deep; deeper for water lilies

Plant List

A. 1 violet-stemmed taro

B. 1 dwarf umbrella palm

C. 1 water lily

D. 5 water lettuce

E. 1 variegated pennywort

F. 1 horsetail

G. 1 water bluebell

Know-How Notes

Water drawn from a water softener is unsuitable to fill a potted water garden. If your water contains chlorine, letting it sit for 24 to 48 hours before planting allows the chemical to evaporate. If your water contains chloramine, you can purchase a product at garden centers to remove the chemical.

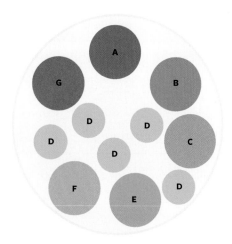

BUILD A BUBBLER

Add a pump to a planter and enjoy the sweet sounds of moving water.

1 SET THE CONTAINER IN PLACE

Set the container where it will receive about 6 hours of sun daily. Rinse the gravel several times to remove residue. Cover the bottom of the pot with 2 inches of gravel. Set the pump-filter-fountain unit in place. Hide the power cord under the gravel.

2 KEEP PLANTS IN POTS

Use a clay-type potting soil, not a lightweight potting mix that contains fertilizer. Cover the top of the soil in each pot with a layer of gravel to hold soil and pots in place.

3 SET POTTED PLANTS IN PLACE

Stage plants on flat rocks or broken bricks, with the top edge of each pot at water level. Add water. Turn on the pump and adjust the fountain height. Add water daily as it evaporates. When the fountain isn't running, use dunk tablets (from a garden center) to control mosquitoes.

Winter Wonderland

Finish the gardening season by filling a generously deep window box with festive elfin shrubs, then enjoy a cheery evergreen landscape right outside your window through fall and winter.

Essentials

Container: 36×11×9-inch cedar window box

Light: Part shade

Water: Apply warm water when the top inch of soil feels dry

Plant List

A. 1 dwarf cedar ('Port Orford')

B. 1 white cedar ('Sunkist')

C. 2 wintercreeper (*Euonymous* 'Emerald Gaiety')

D. 1 winter heather

E. 1 white cedar ('Rheingold')

F. 1 false cypress ('Boulevard')

G. 1 false cypress ('Elwoodii')

H. 1 false cypress ('Hinoki')

Know-How Notes

A layer of mulch slows moisture loss on sunny days. Spray an antidessicant (from a garden center) on evergreens, following product directions, to help prevent damage from winter winds.

Get Ready for the Cold

Make sure the dwarf conifers and other evergreens are winter-hardy in your area. Move the planter to a protected place, when necessary.

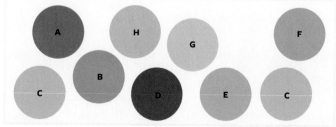

What Goes Around

This dwarf conifer provides an evergreen frame in a potted scheme. Accompanied with other long-season green plants, it produces a textural composition. For special occasions, dress up the greenery by tucking in a small vase of colorful cut flowers.

Essentials

Container: 12-inch wooden planter

Light: Part shade

Water: Keep soil moist

Plant List

A. 1 false cypress ('Ellwoodii')

B. 1 creeping thyme

C. 1 wintercreeper
(*Euonymus* 'Gold Splash')

Know-How Notes

Bring the potted dwarf conifer indoors in fall and use it as a tabletop tree through the holiday season. Keep the plant in a cool room and the soil evenly damp before moving the container back outdoors in spring.

Use a Coaster

Disguise a pot saucer or tray using preserved sheet moss to give the container garden a natural appearance while protecting the surface of a tabletop.

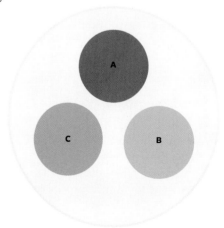

In the Pink

Look to houseplants for a wide selection of dramatically textured and colorful foliage. Group three or five plants with similar needs for light and water, then plant them together in a complementary pot that provides enough room for their growth.

Essentials

Container: 14-inch glazed ceramic pot

Light: Part shade to shade

Water: Keep soil moist

Plant List

A. 1 button fern

B. 1 peacock plant (*Calathea*)

C. 1 pink geranium (Martha Washington)

D. 1 rex begonia

E. 1 pink cyclamen

Boost Humidity

Rex begonias need high humidity and cool shade during hot, dry days of summer. When growing a rex begonia on its own, set the potted plant on a large saucer or tray filled with wet gravel to boost humidity.

Know-How Notes

Keep this potted garden going year-round. Between late summer and fall, place it indoors in a site where it will receive bright, indirect light. Before you let this potted garden vacation outdoors over the summer, remove the geranium from the container and transplant it into a separate pot. All the plants will have more growing room now. Set the potted garden in a place where it will not receive direct sun. Place the geranium in a partly sunny spot.

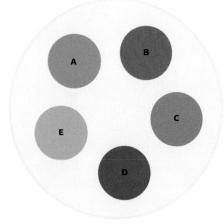

Keeping Romance Alive

Who can resist the allure of an instant garden, let alone one that conjures special effects? Plant this centerpiece in minutes using two colors of the same plant. You'll appreciate its long-lasting beauty as well as the source of glowing candlelight on an outdoor table.

Essentials

Container: 12×12×6-inch flexible stone-veneer planter

Materials: Glass hurricane, taper candle

Light: Part shade to shade

Water: When soil begins to feel dry

Plant List

A. 2 heuchera ('Dolce Mocha Mint')

B. 2 heuchera ('Dolce Key Lime Pie')

Know-How Notes

Choose from a new generation of heuchera—coralbells—with bold-color foliage, vigorous adaptability, and delicious-sounding names for strong additions to long-lasting container gardens. You'll find options with leaf colors including chartreuse, amber, orange, purple, and black.

Superior Perennial

Move the heuchera to the garden at the end of summer. The plants will adapt quickly to garden beds where they get heat and sun, but they will fare best in part shade and cool weather.

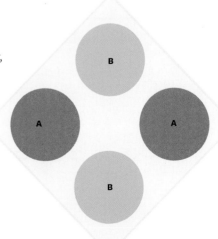

Blue Heaven

Launch the gardening season with this gorgeous scheme. Depending on where you live, start it indoors in late winter or early spring, then move it outdoors once warm weather has come to stay. In late summer, transplant the hydrangea into the garden.

Essentials

Container: 18-inch glazed frostproof pot

Light: Part shade to shade

Water: Keep soil moist

Plant List

A. 1 blue lacecap hydrangea

B. 2 English ivy

C. 2 leatherleaf fern

D. 2 purple viola

E. 1 chartreuse licorice plant

Know-How Notes

Tuck bright green reindeer moss (from a crafts store) between the young plants to heighten the contrast and enhance the garden's overall appeal. As the plants mature, they'll gradually hide the moss.

When to Repot

A hydrangea or other shrub will outgrow its container every two to three years. In early spring, before the plant resumes growth, transplant it into a larger pot to promote growth and flowering. Repot the shrub using fresh potting mix, and water it thoroughly after transplanting.

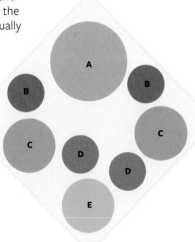

All Dressed Up

Centering a potted garden design on a long-term focal point, such as a dwarf arborvitae, will take it from one season into the next for at least two years. Change the annual underplantings for spring-to-fall then fall-to-spring displays.

Essentials

Container: 18-inch polystyrene planter

Light: Shade

Water: Keep soil moist

Plant List

A. 1 arborvitae

B. 6 pink impatiens

C. 4 blue-purple wishbone flower (*Torenia*)

D. 3 variegated trailing vinca ('Wojo's Jem')

Know-How Notes

Consider a polystyrene (foam) container for your next long-term potted garden. The lightweight, nonporous material will make the garden more portable, less thirsty for water, and less susceptible to temperature extremes.

Leadership Role

It isn't necessary to place the focal-point plant in the center of a potted garden. Think about where the container will be displayed, how it will be viewed, and how the plants will best balance one another. Then plant accordingly.

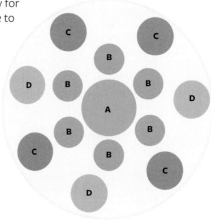

Go Bold with Foliage

A mix of four types of coleus, each tall and with unique color combinations, presents the foliage at center stage in this window box.

Essentials

Container: Window box planter

Light: Part shade

Water: When soil feels dry

Plant List

A. 1 coleus (*Solenostemon* 'Stained Glassworks Copper')

B. 1 lantana 'Dallas Red'

C. 2 beargrass (*Xerophyllum tenax*)

D. 1 coleus (*Solenostemon* 'True Red')

E. 1 coleus (*Solenostemon* 'Stained Glassworks Big Blond')

Know-How Notes

Coleus is one of the most versatile plants for shade, and one of the most colorful. Leaves range from yellow and chartreuse to dark red and purple, with lovely mixes. Coleus is easy to grow and can be rooted at the end of the season so you can enjoy your favorite varieties next year. Just clip stems and set in water. When roots form, plant stems in potting soil.

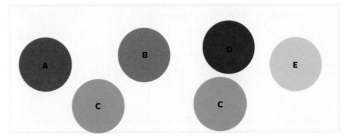

Retaining Moisture

Coleus like moist soil. Make sure your containers are well watered. Retain soil moisture in window boxes and containers by adding mulch at the base of plants. This extra layer over the soil will prevent soil in pots from drying out quickly.

Transition Through the Seasons

Impatiens are a container garden favorite—for good reason: They're long bloomers, they have plenty of color variety, and the foliage stays deep green. They're a proven pick for summer color after springtime violas fade.

Essentials

Container: Window box planter

Light: Shade to partial shade

Water: Keep soil moist

Plant List

A. 3 impatiens ('Dazzler Pink')

B. 3 viola ('Sorbet Blue Babyface')

Know-How Notes

Impatiens add bright color to dark spots. These flowering annuals come in white, pink, coral, red, and bicolors, and they stay in bloom all summer long.

Edible Blooms

Edible viola flowers can be used in sweet and savory dishes. Clip flowers and wash petals, then toss whole flowers into salads, soups, or fritattas. Or dip in egg white then sprinkle sugar over top to make beautiful sugar-coated edible floral cake decorations.

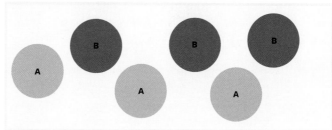

White Elegance

A single color—white—accented with variegated foliage is graceful and beautiful in a simple window box.

Essentials

Container: Window box planter

Light: Partial shade

Water: Keep soil moist

Plant List

A. 1 geranium (*Pelargonium* 'Orbit White')

B. 4 ivy (*Hedera helix* 'Glacier')

C. 3 bacopa (*Sutera* 'Snowstorm')

D. 2 impatiens ('Xtreme White')

Know-How Notes

White gardens, even those in window boxes, add beautiful, quiet, and sophisticated color and texture to outdoor spaces.

Deadheading Tips

Some annuals, such as geraniums, need to have faded blooms removed to encourage new flowers. If the window box is out of deadheading reach, try new geranium varieties, such as Calliope or Caliente, that don't need deadheading to rebloom.

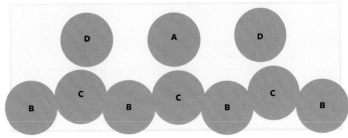

Dress Up a Dormer

Mix bold and unusual foliage, such as kale, sedge, and dark-color coralbells, with flowers in container plantings.

Essentials

Container: Window box planter

Light: Partial shade

Water: Keep soil moist

Plant List

A. 2 sedge (*Carex siderosticha* 'Variegata')

B. 2 kale (*Brassica oleracea* 'Osaka')

C. 2 verbena ('Tuscany Violet with Eye')

D. 2 coralbells (*Heuchera* 'Pewter Moon')

Know-How Notes

Think out of the box when combining plants. Perennials, grasses, and kale are unusual options that work together beautifully.

Perennials in Containers

If you use perennials in window boxes or container plantings, you can remove them at the end of the growing season and transplant them into your garden. If they are hardy in your Zone, they should come back the following spring. Then leave them in the garden or replant in a window box.

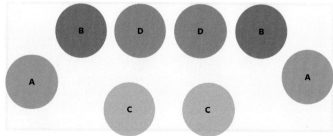

CHAPTER FOUR

Garden Plans

Create the garden of your dreams
with customized plans for shady areas.

Ring Around a Fountain

Make splashing water the cooling focal point of a colorful bed for shade.

A large clay pot, converted into a water feature, is an easy-to-make centerpiece for a simple circular bed. The charming fountain is surrounded with polka-dot plant, an annual that livens up dark parts of the garden with lively splashes of cream and pink.

Impatiens, a shade garden classic available in nearly every hue except blue, adds pizzazz. For a splashier look, mix impatiens of various colors in the bed. Or plant a single color, such as pink, for subdued effect.

Plant these tender annuals in spring after all danger of frost has passed. Impatiens and polka-dot plant like rich soil and plenty of moisture, so work plenty of compost into the soil at planting time. Fertilize with a sprinkling of a slow-release

fertilizer every 4 to 6 weeks during the growing season to maintain profuse flowering.

Although the fountain is an ideal centerpiece, you can substitute your own water feature or garden art. If you prefer, purchase a birdbath or set a statue on a pedestal of stacked bricks or pavers as an alternate center of interest.

The pink in polka-dot plant foliage plays nicely off pink or red impatiens. Or substitute any other colorful shade-loving annuals listed on the opposite page, adjusting the number of plants as needed. Place tall plants closest to the fountain, and encircle them with short plants.

above Round beds look good from every angle

MAKE THIS FOUNTAIN

1. Choose a pot. A plain clay pot works well, or get fancy with a glazed ceramic pot. Also check out fiberglass or resin containers in a variety of shapes.

2. Seal it. If using a clay or ceramic pot, seal the inside of the pot by brushing it with deck sealant. Allow to cure for three days.

3. Choose a pump. Fit the nozzle with a short length of copper pipe (cut to fit), making it as high as the surface of the water will be.

4. Thread the pump cord through the drainage hole in the bottom of the pot (you may need to chip or drill it to make it wider) and seal with exterior caulk.

5. Cure for 1 to 2 days, fill with water, plug in, and enjoy!

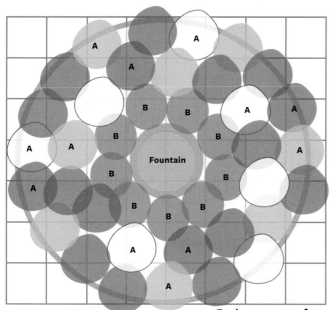

Each square = 1 foot

Plant List

A. 32 impatiens (*Impatiens walleriana*): Annual

B. 9 polka-dot plant (*Hypoestes phyllostachya*): Annual

FIVE SHOWY ANNUALS FOR SHADE

It can be difficult to find colorful annuals for shady areas. Here are some excellent alternatives to the impatiens and polka-dot plants featured in this garden.

Most of these annuals grow best in part shade to full sun in the northernmost quarter of the U.S. They need more shade farther south. They may require full shade in the southern third of the U.S. All need rich soil with ample water and regular fertilization.

1. WISHBONE FLOWER (*Torenia fournieri*) This cup-shape flower grows about 12 inches tall and wide with 1-inch-wide bicolor flowers in shades of blue, purple, pink, or white with a splash of yellow in the throat.

2. BROWALLIA (*Browallia speciosa*) Also called star or sapphire flower, browallia has gorgeous purple-blue or white flowers on plants 12 to 18 inches tall and wide.

3. COLEUS (*Solenostemon scutellarioides*) This plant produces small flower spikes of pale blue or white in late summer, but the flowers are outdone by gorgeous foliage marked in various combinations of green, white, red, burgundy, and yellow. Leaf shapes vary also. Plants grow 12 to 36 inches tall and 12 to 18 inches wide.

4. SCARLET SAGE (*Salvia splendens*) Scarlet sage has large showy flowers in reds, pinks, oranges, creams, or deep purple-red. It does well in full sun or partial shade. This plant likes moisture, and grows up to 2 feet tall and 10 to 15 inches wide.

5. WAX BEGONIA (*Begonia semperflorens*) Also called bedding or fibrous begonia, wax begonia sports shiny green or bronze leaves on plants 8 to 15 inches tall and wide. Clusters of pink, red, or white flowers dangle above the foliage.

A Shaded Strip of Annuals

Nearly every garden has one: a long narrow space next to a building that is cloaked in shade most of the day. Lighten it with flowers.

It's amazing how much pleasure a small well-landscaped space can give, especially if you walk by it every day. Side yards are the perfect example. They are often the neglected stepsisters of the landscape, too often little more than a spot to stash trash cans.

This side yard was magically transformed with simple plantings of colorful annuals and easy-care perennials. The tiny shaded strip close to the house limited planting options, but the combination of impatiens, ferns, tuberous begonias, and columbines has spectacular effect.

Contain the space with a path

The moss-covered brick path keeps the border in bounds. Hanging baskets of fuchsias, tuberous begonias, and variegated vincas contribute to the transformation. Boston ivy (*Parthenocissus tricuspidata*) softens the brick wall with lush green foliage that turns brilliant red in autumn.

In this tiny shaded strip, Christmas ferns are a good choice. They maintain green color nearly year-round, and they won't overwhelm other plantings by spreading. Japanese painted fern (*Athyrium niponicum*), with splashes of silver and maroon, is a showy alternative.

GOOD FERNS GONE BAD

When selecting ferns for small-space beds, look for species such as Christmas fern (*Polystichum acrostichoides*) that won't spread and take over the area. More aggressive species, such as ostrich ferns (*Matteuccia struthiopteris*), spread quickly by underground runners and will choke out other plants in the bed.

left Shade plants thrive even in narrow beds.

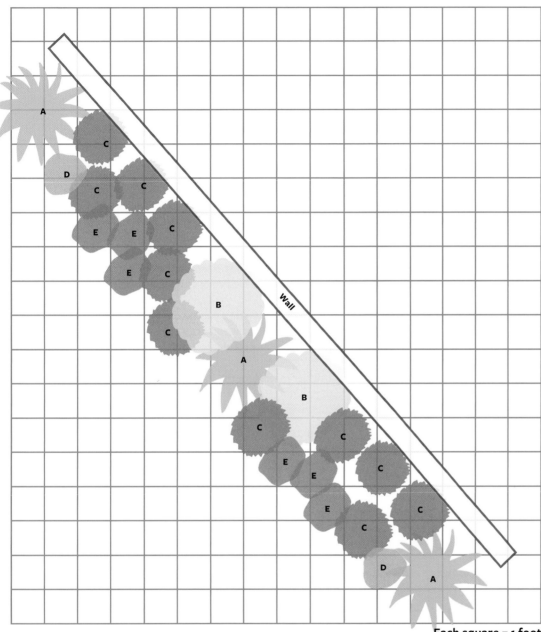

Each square = 1 foot

Plant List

A. **3 Christmas fern** (*Polystichum acrostichoides*): Zones 3–9

B. **2 columbine** (*Aquilegia × hybrida*): Zones 3–9

C. **11 impatiens** (*Impatiens walleriana*): Annual

D. **2 tuberous begonia** (*Begonia × tuberhybrida*): Annual

E. **6 wishbone flower** (*Torenia fournieri*): Annual

Plant a Circle of Color

So little sun that grass won't grow? Put in a bright bed of flowers instead!

Mature trees are a mixed blessing. They provide restful shade, but grass won't grow well under their leafy canopies. One solution: Blanket the ground with colorful annuals that thrive where turf won't. This garden is filled with brilliant red wax begonias (you could substitute impatiens) close to the tree, where shade is deepest. The edge of the bed that receives more sun has subdued color from dusty millers, ageratums, and lobelias.

Boxwoods provide a permanent anchor to the planting. Annual flowers are unequaled at providing season-long color, but if you prefer perennials, consider substituting reblooming fringed bleeding heart (*Dicentra eximia*) for the wax begonias and hardy geraniums for the lobelias and ageratums. Both perennials can provide color all summer. Hostas in various shades of green, white, and gold could substitute for the dusty miller.

Tips for planting around trees

Planting around the base of a tree helps the tree blend into the overall landscape. Follow these tips to plant flowers next to trees:

Determine how much shade the tree casts. Some trees with high, open canopies and small leaves, such as honey locust, create little shade, while others with dense, low-hanging branches, such as spruce, create deep shade.

Assess the available soil moisture. Some trees, such as maples, are notorious for sucking moisture from the soil under their boughs. Grow drought-tolerant plants around moisture-hogging trees.

Add no soil over tree roots. Tempting as it may be to build a raised bed around a tree, burying roots with even a few inches of soil can kill a sensitive tree.

Dig with caution. It's OK to slice through a few small roots with a trowel, but avoid cutting roots that are thicker than an inch in diameter.

Play around with pots. An easy way to grow flowers under trees with problematic soil is to tuck in several pots filled with colorful shade-loving annuals.

Get edgy. Install some type of edging around the bed to prevent turf from creeping in. You'll make maintenance even easier.

above A mass of begonias are encircled by dusty miller, boxwoods, ageratums, and lobelia.

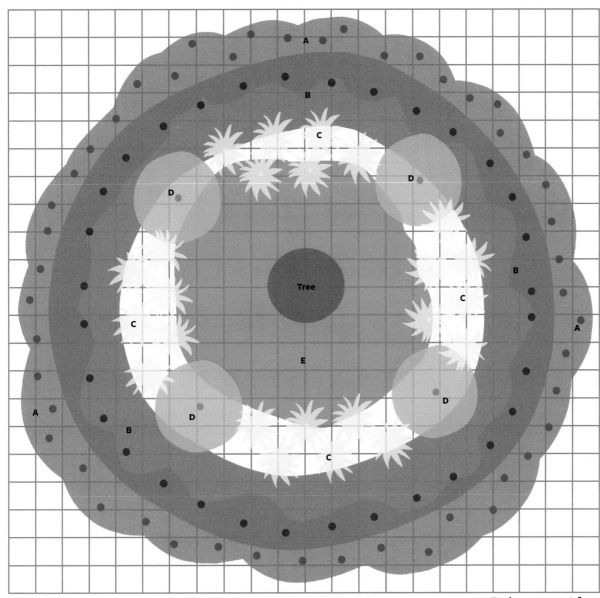

Each square = 1 foot

Plant List

A. 48 edging lobelia (*Lobelia erinus*): Annual

B. 32 ageratum (*Ageratum houstonianum*): Annual

C. 24 dusty miller (*Senecio cineraria*): Zones 8–10, annual elsewhere

D. 4 boxwood (*Buxus* sp.): Zones 5–7

E. 28 red wax begonia (*Begonia × semperflorens*): Annual

Easy Perennials for Light Shade

Care for those spots that fall between sun and shade with simple flowers that come back year after year.

Do you have an area with partial shade that you'd like to fill with minimal-care perennials? Then this is your garden. The marvelous mix of pretty perennials offers blooms in purple, pink, and chartreuse. All perennials in this garden thrive in light shade—4 to 6 hours of direct, unfiltered morning (or late afternoon) sun a day or dappled shade most of the day. Likely locations for such light conditions are under the canopy of a high tree or next to large shrubs or a building that blocks afternoon sun.

Expand your plan to fit your space

Plant this small garden by itself, or extend the color show with bright pink astilbes planted at one end and pink snapdragons at the other end. The plants featured in this garden need ample moisture. If you plant them under a tree with shallow roots, such as a maple, you'll need to provide supplemental water.

If you love to take cut flowers into your home, this garden offers a bonus: All the blooms in this plan excel in bouquets. If you have room, extend the garden on each end to grow your favorite cutting flowers. You won't miss the flowers, and the excess will ensure pretty flowers to enjoy indoors for at least a couple of months of the year.

left Too shady for grass? Use shade plants to replace a thread-bare lawn.

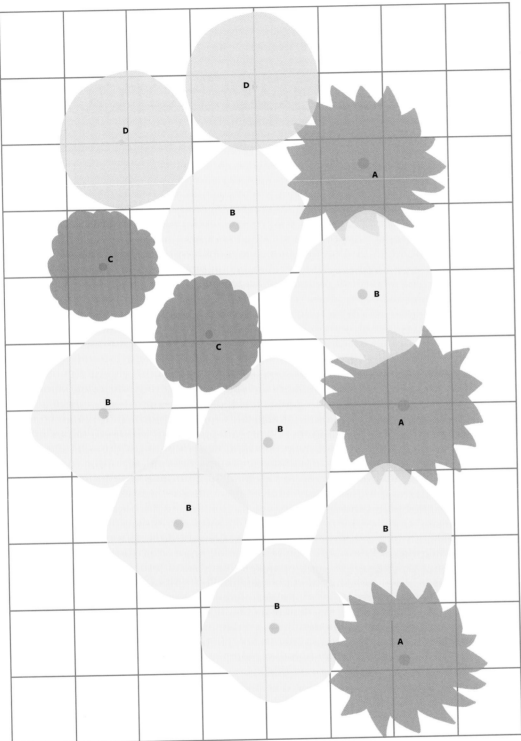

Plant List

A. 3 hyssop (*Hyssopus officinalis*): Zones 6–9

B. 7 lady's mantle (*Alchemilla mollis*): Zones 4–7

C. 2 hardy geranium (*Geranium* 'Rozanne'): Zones 4–8

D. 2 bleeding heart (*Dicentra spectabilis*): Zones 4–8

Each square = 1 foot

A Soothing Shady Border

Cool, green, and refreshing, this low-key planting for full shade is restful and elegant.

Embrace the subtle gradations of foliage colors, textures, and shapes by tending a peaceful shade garden. Gardeners with limited sun often are frustrated because they can't grow the wide variety of plants with showy flowers that is possible with more light. However, over time most shade gardeners readjust their expectations to appreciate the beautiful foliage, distinctive plant shapes, subtle colors, soft-hue flowers, and textural differences among shade-tolerant plants.

This plan is a delightful place to begin to appreciate shade. It highlights a variety of foliage plants, from beautiful, fragrant spring flowers of azalea to the delicate foliage of fringed bleeding heart to the bold, architectural foliage of hosta. The plants in this shade garden grow best in moist, loamy soil. If your garden soil is less desirable, work in compost at planting time to help retain moisture and nutrients.

below Layer shade plants of varying heights for the most dramatic effect.

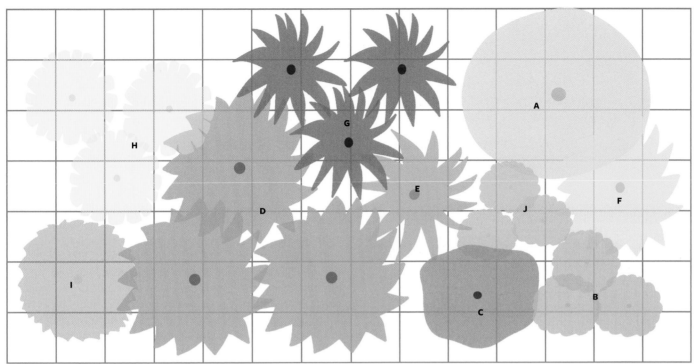

Each square = 1 foot

Plant List

A. 1 azalea (*Rhododendron* sp.) Zones 4–9

B. 3 fringed bleeding heart (*Dicentra exima*): Zones 4–8

C. 1 Virginia knotweed (*Persicaria virginiana*): Zones 5–9

D. 3 fragrant hosta (*Hosta plantaginea*) or other medium-large hostas: Zones 3–8

E. 1 variegated hybrid hosta (*Hosta* sp.) such as 'Patriot': Zones 3–8

F. 1 narrow-spiked ligularia (*Ligularia stenocephala* 'The Rocket'): Zones 4–8

G. 3 Solomon's seal (*Polygonatum commutatum*): Zones 3–8

H. 3 yellow foxglove (*Digitalis grandiflora*): Zones 3–8

I. 1 old-fashioned bleeding heart (*Dicentra spectabilis*): Zones 3–9

J. 3 hybrid anemone (*Anemone* × *hybrida*): Zones 4–8

BHG TEST GARDEN TIP

MULCH GENEROUSLY

Mulch is especially important in a moisture-loving shade garden such as this one. Apply 1 to 3 inches, refreshing each spring.

Hostas by a Fountain

What could be more cooling—or cooler—than a water feature surrounded by moisture-loving hostas?

above Hostas love shade and moisture, perfect for a fountain garden.

Water and shade are a natural pairing. They bring to mind babbling brooks and leafy riversides. Re-create that feeling in your own backyard. The centerpiece of this evocative garden is a millstone fountain. Millstone replica versions are readily available at many garden centers. Or you can substitute a different ready-made fountain kit. Just set it up, fill with water, plug it in, and enjoy! (Note: You'll need a GFCI outdoor electrical source for the fountain. Have an electrician install a GFCI outlet near the desired fountain location. As the plants grow, they will hide the electrical source.)

Soften edges with color and texture

Surround the fountain with a variety of hostas. The plan suggests specific cultivars, but you can mix and match with your favorites. The key is to include a range of colors (yellow-green, variegated green and white, blue-green) and textures (smooth, crinkled, and curled leaves).

Smaller, variegated types of wintercreeper make an excellent low-maintenance edging. However, be sure to plant a cultivar that grows no more than 2 feet high and 2 feet wide, such as 'Emerald 'n' Gold' and some types of 'Green 'n' Gold' (check the label to be certain on size). Other types of wintercreeper can get 5 or 6 feet high and wide.

Alternative shade-tolerant edging plants include impatiens, lady's mantle, bergenia, and fringed bleeding heart.

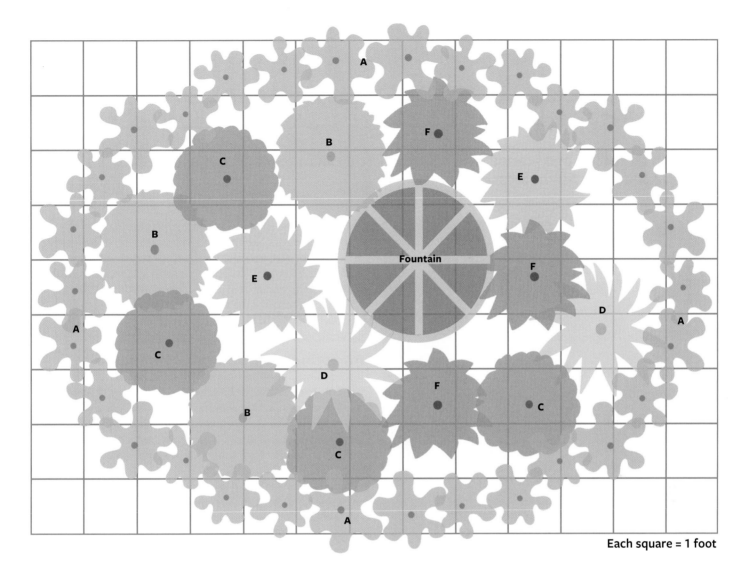

Each square = 1 foot

Plant List

A. 30 small-growing wintercreeper (*Euonymous fortunei*): Zones 5–9

B. 3 green-and-white variegated hosta ('Night Before Christmas'): Zones 3–8

C. 4 blue-green hosta, ('Halcyon'): Zones 3–8

D. 2 yellow-green hosta with blue-green splashes ('Tokudama Aureonebulosa'): Zones 3–8

E. 2 gold hosta with blue-green edging ('Paul's Glory'): Zones 3–8

F. 3 fragrant hostas (*Hosta plantaginea*): Zones 3–8

A Garden by the Woods

This shade-loving bed transitions perfectly from lawn to woods. It's ideal for just about any low-light location.

above A series of colorful birdhouses adds fun to a shady border.

Seamlessly blend a manicured lawn with towering trees by planting a pleasant, curving strip of perennials. The boundary between a wooded area and lawn can be challenging to landscape. A formal flowerbed looks artificial juxtaposed with the wild of the woods. And a casual planting can look like an unkempt extension of the wooded area.

This border is the ideal solution. It's filled with plants that naturally do well in the partial shade near mature trees.

Add whimsical structural elements

Birdhouses on posts add vertical accents to the bed, mimicking tree trunks that form the backdrop to the garden. The bird abodes further tame the planting, indicating a human touch. Boulders dug from elsewhere on the property are positioned to serve as natural sculptures. If your property is stone-free, find rocks from another local source, or substitute additional plants or garden ornaments.

This border would also look good next to a tall fence or alongside a building that casts light shade.

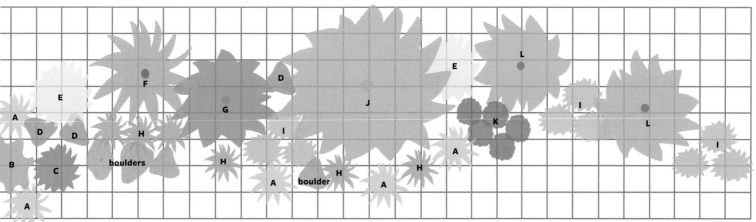

Each square = 1 foot

Plant List

A. 5 yellow-green hybrid hosta ('Piedmont Gold'): Zones 3–8

B. 1 blue-green hosta ('Hadspen Blue'): Zones 3–8

C. 1 green with gold edge hosta ('Golden Tiara'): Zones 3–8

D. 3 caladium (*Caladium bicolor*): Zones 8–11, annual elsewhere

E. 2 yellow-green hosta with blue-green edge ('Captain Kirk'): Zones 3–8

F. 1 siebold hosta (*Hosta sieboldiana*): Zones 3–8

G. 1 blue-green hosta with gold edges ('Tokudama Flavocircinalis'): Zones 3–8

H. 6 lungwort (*Pulmonaria saccharata*) ('Mrs. Moon'): Zones 4–8

I. 9 woodland phlox (*Phlox divaricata*): Zones 4–9

J. 1 cutleaf Japanese maple (*Acer palmatum* 'Dissectum Rubrifolium'): Zones 6–8

K. 5 impatiens (*Impatiens walleriana*): Annual

L. 2 large yellow-green hosta ('Sum and Substance'): Zones 3–8

TIPS FOR LANDSCAPING NEAR WOODLANDS

Step up with shrubs. Shrubs and small landscape trees help the eye to visually adjust to taller woodland trees. A border of shrubs is extremely effective in blending cultivated areas with woodland.

Go natural. Accent the garden with nature-theme accessories. The birdhouses and stones in this garden are excellent examples. Also consider bee skeps, decorative bird feeders, driftwood, or small statues of woodland animals.

Outsmart the animals. Rather than fighting deer and rabbits, select and plant flowers and shrubs that animals find less tasty and are more likely to leave alone.

Shade Pocket Garden

Even the tiniest corner of a backyard can become a jewel box of color. Caladiums, hostas, and impatiens fit snugly in this garden nook.

Nearly every yard has one—a dark corner tucked away where nothing but weeds seem to grow. Fix it!

It could be a spot by a back door, a niche between garage and house, or a forlorn corner of yard that cries out for sprucing up. Fill it will colorful shade-loving plants that are easy to grow.

Two large hostas dominate the back of this planting. Even when the hostas lack flowers, the foliage is attractive. If you choose hostas that have leaf edges variegated in yellow, cream, or white, the planting will pop even more.

Caladiums also play a key role in this bed. Few plants adapted to shade are wildly colorful, and caladiums are a standout that thrives in summer heat and humidity. Although they are perennial only in Zones 10 and 11, gardeners in colder areas can save the cost of replacing them annually by digging up tubers in the fall and storing them over winter. Another cost-saving idea: Substitute coleus for the caladiums. They provide color at a fraction of the cost.

left Create colorful drama by adding small to tall shade-loving plants in a small secluded bed.

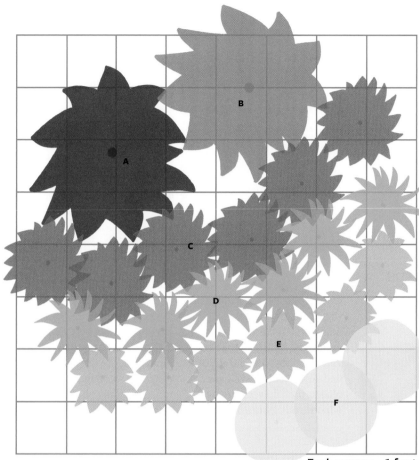

Each square = 1 foot

Plant List

A. 1 green hosta with white edge ('Regal Splendor'): Zones 3–8

B. 1 green hosta with gold edge ('Yellow River'): Zones 3–8

C. 6 red caladium (*Caladium bicolor*) ('Florida Cardinal'): Zones 10–11, annual elsewhere

D. 6 chartreuse caladium with red flecks (*Caladium bicolor*) ('Miss Muffet'): Zones 10–11, annual elsewhere

E. 6 lungwort (*Pulmonaria saccharata*): Zones 4–8

F. 3 impatiens (*Impatiens walleriana*): Zones 10–11, annual elsewhere

PLANT SUPERSTAR: CALADIUM

Caladiums look like the exotic tropical plants they are. In their native Central and South America, they grow on the banks of rain forest streams in gorgeous swaths of color. Their big arrow-shape leaves have vivid markings, often speckled or veined, in pinks, greens, reds, silvers, and whites. Dwarf types grow just a foot tall, while tall types can reach 3 feet. Leaves can be as small as 6 inches or as long as 2 feet.

Caladiums are available in the spring as established plants in pots or as tubers. Most varieties prefer at least afternoon shade, though some newer types tolerate sun. Provide plenty of water (1 inch or more per week) to actively growing plants. Caladiums prefer loose, moist soil, so work in plenty of compost at planting time.

Caladiums come back year after year in subtropical regions (Zones 10 to 11). They won't tolerate frost. In colder regions, treat them as annuals and let them die back in fall. Or to save the cost of replacing them next year, dig up the caladium tubers after the first frost. Remove soil from the tubers, and store them indoors in sawdust or dry peat moss in a cool (60ºF) location. Pot the tubers in late winter to get a head start on spring planting.

Top Perennial Picks

Choose flowering perennials that fit the type of shade in your yard.

above Mass colorful shade lovers, such as astilbe, to brighten shaded spots.

PARTIAL TO FULL SHADE

Ajuga (*Ajuga reptans*) With dozens of cultivars available, this pretty groundcover makes a striking show with variegated foliage in tones of green, white, pink, burgundy, and silver. It also produces blue or pink flowers; grows 6 inches tall. Zones 3–9

Astilbe (*Astilbe* sp.) This plant's ferny foliage and feathery plumes have made it a favorite. Many types are available, in colors such as pink, white, red, lavender, and peach. Grows 6 inches to 3 feet tall, depending on species. Zones 4–9

LIGHT SHADE

Columbine (*Aquilegia* hybrids) This spring-blooming native with intricate spurred flowers grows 1 to 4 feet tall. Some types reseed freely. Zones 3–9

Daylily (*Hemerocallis* hybrids) Choose from tall (up to 4 feet) or miniature forms (as short as 1 foot). 'Stella de Oro' is one of the most popular minis. Main bloom is midsummer. Some rebloom several times each year if deadheaded diligently. Zones 3–9

Below are excellent picks for perennial plants that thrive in partial to full shade, as long as they also get ample moisture.

Azure Monkshood
(*Aconitum carmichaelii*)
Resembling delphinium, this perennial produces spikes of beautiful deep blue flowers in early fall. It grows 4 to 6 feet tall. Zones 3–7

Bleeding Heart
Old-fashioned bleeding heart (*Dicentra spectablis*) sends forth spectacular arches of heart-shape blooms in pink and white in spring then its foliage dies back.
Zones 3–9

Yellow Corydalis
(*Corydalis lutea*) One of the longest bloomers among shade-loving plants, this plant produces yellow flowers from spring through fall. Needs ample moisture and good drainage. Grows to 16 inches tall. Zones 5–8

Spiderwort (*Tradescantia* sp.) This plant with grassy foliage produces clusters of blue, purple, or white flowers on stems that grow up to 3 feet tall. Zones 4–9

Light shade, which is 4 to 6 hours of direct, unfiltered light a day in the South; 6 hours in the northern half of the U.S. where the sun is less intense. Daylily, coralbells, and columbine tolerate even dry shade.

Blue False Indigo
(*Baptisia australis*) Gorgeous blue flowers appear on spikes in late spring. The attractive blue-green foliage grows 3 to 5 feet tall, depending on light and moisture. Stake to prevent flopping. Zones 3–9

Coralbells (*Heuchera* hybrids) Leaves of coralbells earn nearly equal billing as the sprays of pink, coral, or white flowers. Foliage can be medium green, yellow-green, deep purple, silver-streaked, or variegated. Grows about 12 inches tall and wide; flower spikes reach 16 to 30 inches. Zones 3–8

Obedient Plant
(*Physostegia virginiana*) This spreading moisture-lover grows 1 to 4 feet tall with spikes of white or pink in midsummer to fall. Can be somewhat invasive in ideal conditions. Zones 2–9

CHAPTER FIVE

Living the Shady Life

Discover how creative homeowners turn shaded spots into lush and verdant landscapes.

Shaded Sanctuary

A wooded landscape and natural-looking pond bring a sense of mystery and delight to an urban property.

As you step into this tree-filled backyard just outside St. Louis, the stress-inducing sounds of city life fade away, replaced by the gentle murmurs of a trickling stream. Rock walls and terraces installed by a previous owner blend into a harmonious whole with the soothing pond, garden beds, and container plantings added by the current homeowner. If you long for an escape from the hectic pace of life, use these strategies to transform your urban setting into a countrylike retreat.

Add trees for privacy. Seventy-foot-tall bald cypress trees (*Taxodium distichum*) stand guard above the rest of the garden, creating a sense of shelter, adding shade on hot summer days, and gently blocking out the rest of the world. Without this framework of trees, the garden would feel exposed to city bustle and neighboring properties.

Create a natural-looking water feature. Here, a waterway is created out of the yard's natural slope, then wood from several dead or dying trees is used for accents. Several moss-covered logs—some with plants growing from crevices in the wood—sit in the streambed, an illusion of having a long-standing history.

Accent with containers. In this garden with timeworn appeal, intriguing container plantings blend dramatic combinations of tropicals, annuals, and perennials. Containers of coleus, 'Margarita' sweet potato vine (*Ipomoea batatas*), golden creeping Jenny (*Lysimachia nummularia* 'Aurea'), and Wave petunias bring welcome color and texture to pockets of space.

opposite Stone walls and vinyl shake shingles lend a rustic atmosphere to this property just 5 miles from downtown St. Louis. **right** Annuals casually mix with tropical favorites such as sweet potato vine in creative container plantings.

opposite An outdoor work space charmingly displays collectibles adjacent to the pond. **above** A 1950s bike with a handlebar basket stands in to display seasonal color. The rustic bike can be moved around the gardens and get seasonal uplifts.

left Logs placed in the pond give the new water feature a been-there-forever appearance. At the border, large clumps of *Gunnera manicata* add impressive foliage to the woodsy scene. **above** Allium 'Globemaster' lends its distinctive spherical form to a sunny pocket near the garden stream.

Color Up

This foliage-filled backyard in the Pacific Northwest sparkles with fall hues.

It's challenging to increase landscape color in shaded areas of the Pacific Northwest. Under the canopy of large trees, Douglas fir, evergreens, hemlock, and western red cedar, these homeowners sought plants to enliven—even in the shade. Here's how they did it.

Pack beds. A small rectangular front entryway garden has all the right stuff: focal point, water feature, trees, perennials, and grasses. Filled with plants of varying size, texture, and hues, this small-space garden has appeal in all seasons.

Repeat elements. Fuchsia adds dots and dashes of vibrant color throughout the landscape. Textural Japanese hakone grass provides a flowing shape and is used in beds and containers to create continuity.

Stairstep containers. The mix of small, medium, and large plants and containers creates a layered effect of texture and colors, lined up like choir members by height. So easy!

Mimic nature. Planter combinations mirror the natural landscape of the nearby Pacific Northwest woods. Frilly ferns in a stone container grow beneath the elegant arching branches of Japanese maple.

Mix it up. The homeowners combined a variety of leaf color, shape, and texture as well as flower color and bloom times.

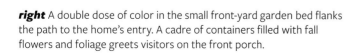

right A double dose of color in the small front-yard garden bed flanks the path to the home's entry. A cadre of containers filled with fall flowers and foliage greets visitors on the front porch.

above Fall foliage has naturally gorgeous combos. *Aralia elata* leaves morph from green to gold as temperatures drop. Flowering kale resemble clusters of roses and hold their hues even after frost. ***left*** Stone outcroppings and a center-stage fire pit add natural elements to the side-yard garden. Fire adds the right light for intimate evenings with friends and family and a hot spot to toast marshmallows.

The stacked stone wall adds rustic appeal to the landscape while providing a spot to showcase pots of plants. Walls can also be used for seating.

left The seating area is snugged up against the street—but you'd never know it. Open-design wooden fencing panels and shrubs create privacy, screen the view, and allow filtered light without a boxed-in feeling. *top* Pyracantha features red, yellow, or orange berries in autumn. *above* The heart-shape crimson leaves of redbud hazel (*Disanthus cercidifolius*) add vibrant, almost pulsating color to shaded spots. This understory tree grows 6 to 8 feet tall.

Sweet Seclusion

Surrounding your home with plants creates a private retreat.

A grove of trees, a swath of shrubs, and a bevy of flowering plants transition between home and garden—and garden and neighborhood. Creating privacy in your yard is as simple as planting a buffer. Restrict views and muffle street traffic or neighborhood sounds with plantings. That's what homeowners did in this yard near downtown Raleigh, North Carolina. The wraparound fence of view-blocking vegetation and large shade trees provide privacy and fabulous views on three sides of this property.

The landscape reaps the benefits of seasonal color with flowers in the spring and dense green in the winter. The perimeter of the yard is almost impenetrable from view in summer. Tall shade trees, small ornamental trees, shrubs of all sizes, perennials, and groundcovers are coordinated to form a dense wall to mask views of the surrounding streets and traffic sounds. In winter, when deciduous plants lose leaves, broadleaf evergreens such as rhododendrons, camellias, wax myrtle, and boxwood form a green screen.

Gently curving garden beds are islands of color in the sea of green grass inside the living fence. Bold strokes of annuals, visible from the house and outdoor gathering areas, decorate the private Eden for weeks during the summer. Beds in the interior of the yard feature plants of varying heights that create visual interest. The organization and placement of the beds of blooms also form distinct areas inside the yard, making it feel more spacious. Separate seating and dining areas give the sense of multiple rooms within the green space.

right Pressure-treated wooden decking forms a clean pathway between house and garden. The walkway also gives the beds sharply defined edges—a geometric counterpoint to the exuberant plantings.

Sweet Seclusion

There are many ways you can plant for privacy. One is to raise the profile of plantings through elevation. Give plants view-blocking power in raised beds or berms. A foot or two of extra height lets large plants act as screens. Planting in slightly elevated spaces places medium-size plants at eye level.

Another way to add seclusion to landscapes is to grow trees, shrubs, and perennials in layers, creating a sheltered yard to block views from neighbors. Make an extra-secluded yard by layering plantings to form pockets where you can't see your house or another part of the yard. You'll feel as if you're getting away from it all in your own garden. Creating secluded areas within your yard gives you separate spaces for various activities. For example, when entertaining, you could serve drinks in one area and a sit-down dinner in another.

If you don't want to make an entire yard a private paradise, transform one corner into a secluded getaway. Carefully place a couple of trees to form a pocket of seclusion; a spot to enjoy morning coffee or an after-work glass of wine.

The classic way to create a green screen is to plant a hedge. Look for evergreen varieties to provide year-round screening, or try types that lose leaves in winter then make up for it by putting on a show with attractive spring or summer flowers or a blaze of fall color. While many plants are suitable as hedges, yours will be a cinch to care for if you select a variety adapted to your climate and that matures at the height and width you want a hedge to be. For small areas, look for columnar shrubs—those that grow up rather than out. For large areas, choose wider-growing shrubs.

opposite Planting beds hold closely knit swaths of bright annuals, while shade-loving perimeter shrubs and trees have loose, unpruned character. **above right** Shade-loving impatiens and Japanese maple add color and texture to the house foundation. **right** A bed of layered shrubs offers seclusion and lushness.

opposite The backyard deck seems to float above dark pink impatiens. The view from this area sweeps across the dense border that encloses the property. **above** A gently curving path of limestone and gravel, with natural-looking and carefree presence, leads from driveway to house.

Space to Entertain

Share a garden's beauty with friends and family by shaping a landscape full of potential to host gatherings. This Ohio garden does just that with distinct entertainment areas.

Neighborhood barbecues in the summer. Casual family dinners. An early-morning cup of tea. It's all possible in a well-planned garden. Create opportunities to relax with friends by providing plenty of places to sit and tables to hold food. This garden goes an extra step with three separate outdoor rooms: kitchen, dining space, and living room. Each room is clearly defined and maintains the character of the overall garden. These tips are useful for making an outdoor space worthy of a gathering for friends.

Establish spaces. Whether you have one or three areas to enjoy outdoor meals, set entertainment areas apart from the rest of the garden with structured elements with low walls or simple fences. If you want borders to be more open, a simple stone patio is enough to distinguish a dining area. In this garden, a combination of stone walls and white fences outlines structured borders for the three rooms.

Outfit the area for entertaining. At the most low-maintenance level, provide plenty of chairs and tables for guests. This garden is equipped with everything for a successful meal, from food preparation to lounging after dinner. In the kitchen area, a stainless-steel grill and sink are built into the stone wall. A large table and several chairs in the dining area provide ample space for guests to enjoy a meal. Later, they can proceed to the living room area to lounge on love seats.

Unify spaces. Although they're separate areas with different purposes, maintain the sense of one garden by keeping materials and plants consistent from space to space. In this garden, neutral tones appear throughout on the stone walls and white fences. All the furniture is understated creams, browns, or greens, while roses and hostas grace the borders of each room.

opposite A simple table set establishes the dining area's purpose. A small fountain near the wall provides soothing background sounds while guests enjoy a meal. **right** 'Patriot' hostas and boxwood shrubs divided by cobblestone-look walkways lead on a meandering path to the house.

above The classic white fence stands out against a blend of flowers, including bright red roses, and variegated hostas. **_opposite_** Flowers peek through the fence in this secluded sitting area. The spot is perfect for taking in the relaxing color and fragrance.

above Containers with shade-loving annuals, hosta, and boxwood help soften the angular lines of the kitchen area. **opposite** Boston ferns add instant green lushness to shaded areas. These easy-care plants are available at garden centers in spring and summer. Bring them indoors as houseplants in areas that receive frost.

left The archway and scalloped fencing distinguish the living area from the rest of the backyard. Cobblestone edging, a unifying factor in the garden, frames the landscaping. **top** Plantings are consistent from room to room and include roses, peonies, irises, and 'Patriot' hostas. **above** Terra-cotta planters scattered throughout the garden display combinations that thrive in each space.

Country Garden Dreamer

Love, labor, and truckloads of compost turn stony Pennsylvania clay into an oasis for people and birds.

If you were to choose a site for creating a dream garden, a rocky, clay former cornfield probably wouldn't rank high on your list of ideal possibilities. But when gardening is in your blood, as it is for Kathy Engle, you learn to work with what you have. With a lot of love, a lot of energy, and a lot of compost (hauled by husband Don), Kathy transformed a half acre of suburban Pennsylvania lawn into a flower-filled paradise.

Kathy began more than 20 years ago with great intentions of organized design, crafting a detailed map for the planting of her first 10×25-foot border. That plan lasted barely a year before she jumped into moving plants around, expanding the border, and planting new areas. Now her Shippensburg home is surrounded by about 1,400 feet of free-form beds and borders packed with more than 300 kinds of flowers, vines, shrubs, and trees. The gardens connect via a network of winding grass and paved paths that invite visitors to stroll and explore.

right Named for its key feature, Kathy Engle's Arbor Garden is packed with colorful flowering and foliage plants for all-season interest. The show really explodes with color during autumn with an abundance of mums, asters, sedums, grasses, and hydrangeas.

Country Garden Dreamer

One of Kathy's priorities is planning and planting for multiseason interest. "More than anything else," she says, "I've worked hard to make sure my gardens are in bloom from 'swing up to swing down,' from spring bulbs to October mums and asters." Fragrance is another trait she looks for in new plants—especially those destined to grow near her favorite sitting areas, such as the shady spot near her white-painted backyard arbor.

Color speaks to Kathy's heart, too, and her garden reflects that with a rich palette of pinks, blues, yellows, and greens. Touches of white in painted swings, chairs, fences, posts, and tuteurs, as well as hydrangeas, phlox, Shasta daisies (*Leucanthemum* × *superbum* 'Becky'), and other white flowers accent these hues.

Kathy's eye for choosing and placing an eclectic collection of ornaments gives this garden its true country charm. Ornament style ranges from classic to rustic to whimsical, and they all fit perfectly into the surroundings—photoworthy vignettes throughout the landscape. Even better, many decorative accents double as functional features. More than 20 quaint and colorful birdhouses, for example, provide shelter for a variety of winged visitors that call the garden home. When they first moved to the property, Kathy and Don saw no birds; now a chirping chorus serves as a natural alarm clock on summer mornings.

above left Draped with a tablecloth crocheted by Kathy's mother, the backyard bistro table is a delightful spot for summer entertaining. ***left*** Colorful 'Cotton Candy' agastache and 'Patricia Ballard' asters provide nectar for butterflies. ***above*** Kathy holds a freshly cut daisy. ***opposite*** Sheltered under the spreading branches of an oak tree, Kathy's backyard pond is home to a growing population of fish and frogs, as well as a variety of water lilies, water hyacinths, and pickerel weed.

ADD A PERSONAL TOUCH

Are you stuck with a less-than-gorgeous garden shed? With a little ingenuity, you can turn an ordinary prefab into a personality-packed feature for your country garden.

Fit it with trim. Check out your local home improvement center's selection of decorative trim pieces. Choose a few that strike your fancy, paint or stain them, and use them to spruce up the structure.

Have fun with color. A little paint can go a long way toward giving a shed a fresh look. Pick the same colors as your house to visually link the two; choose a few of your favorite flower colors so the shed complements your plantings.

Be an exterior decorator. Have fun dressing up a drab shed with a collection of quaint objects, such as wreaths, signs, or old garden tools.

Plant it up. Turn the shed itself into a garden! Tack plastic netting to the sides and let morning glories or clematis climb up and over it; add a few brackets to the corners for hanging baskets. And remember window boxes: Hang them on the walls if there are no windows.

opposite above Set among expansive mixed borders, the Garden House is a focal point in this backyard haven. **opposite, far left** Songbirds are drawn to a variety of birdhouses throughout the garden. **opposite middle** A Monarch butterfly sits on a 'Pink Delight' butterfly bush (*Buddleja davidii*). **opposite right** The pink roof of this birdhouse is the perfect color echo for 'Autumn Joy' sedum and 'Anthony Waterer' spirea. **above** Gourds find a perfect perch on a rustic rocking chair. **above right** A texture-rich combination of foam flower (*Tiarella* 'Iron Butterfly'), Japanese painted fern (*Athyrium niponicum* var. *pictum*), and 'Pia' hydrangea.

Little Charmers

Mini hostas focus the beauty and infinite variability of big hostas in tiny, irresistible treasures.

When the object of your affection is a miniature hosta, there's little question about the nature of the attraction: These pocket-size hostas are simply cute. "They are just adorable," says Marsha Ansevics, who grows more than 70 mini hosta varieties at Flying Frog Farms, the retail and mail-order nursery she started eight years ago—just days after retiring as a high school science teacher. "They have an adorable little leaf—all the patterns of the big hostas, just down to such a tiny little scale," she says.

Marsha and her husband, Bruno, specialize in hostas of all sizes; they grow about a thousand varieties under big pine trees and in 10 shade houses on their 20-acre property in Indianola, Iowa, just south of Des Moines. Mini hostas—officially, those that grow 4 to 6 inches tall and have leaves of only about 4 square inches—are among Marsha's favorites.

Marvelous miniature hostas can be as ruffled, rounded, puckered, or painterly as big ones, but you can grow them in a teacup. They're sparkling little charmers at the front of a flowerbed, but they're especially winsome and irresistible in pots, on their own, or with small ferns or coralbells (*Heuchera*), also known for colorful leaves. Insatiable hosta collectors like miniature varieties because the plants are an opportunity to grow dozens of cultivars in smaller plots.

"Everyone loves hostas because they grow in shade, they need little care, and there are so many of them, you can grow them together like a pretty tapestry," Marsha says. She has customers who want to grow one of each kind and others who experiment with only blue-leaf hostas or hostas with yellow variegation. Visitors to Flying Frog Farms see dozens of tiny hostas at the fronts of shade gardens, holding their own against the spectacular displays of specimen hostas that grow up to 8 feet across.

opposite Marsha Ansevics of Flying Frog Farms holds one of her favorite mini hostas, 'Silver Threads and Golden Needles'. **right** Deep green hostas turn the wooded nursery into a lush forest. Marsha is the owner and "head frog" of this nursery in Indianola, Iowa, named for the prolific leopard frogs that live on the property.

Little Charmers

Mini hostas have charming names: 'Baby Bunting', one of the first minis introduced, in 1982, has little heart-shape green leaves and lavender flowers. 'Blue Mouse Ears' has cupped, silvery blue leaves; 'Bitsy Gold' grows to form an 18-inch-wide clump, only 6 inches tall, with strappy golden leaves. The captivating 'Pandora's Box', which Marsha says can be difficult to grow, is the smallest variegated hosta: It is only about 3 inches tall. Like many hostas with a touch of white, it needs sun, but not too much.

These tiny hostas sometimes carry big price tags. Marsha says she and Bruno have paid close to $100 for a single hosta, but they don't do it often. The newest minis might cost $50 or more. "When I hit $20 I always think it is quite a bit," she says. Pretty little 'Dixie Chickadee', which has creamy-yellow leaves edged in dark green and only grows to about 4 inches tall, sells for $16 and up. 'Baby Bunting' remains one of the most popular minis and can often be found for about $5.

Miniature hostas grow quickly, even in this Zone 5 garden. A plant that starts out only 3 inches across will spread to about 6 inches in just a year and keep growing, Marsha says. "Just let them spread—they won't get taller," she says. You could also divide plants to share with friends. These little charmers will not outgrow their spots, but you might find yourself making room for more of them in your garden because they will likely claim a big space in your heart.

above left Marsha and Bruno dig up a big 'Sun Power' hosta. Hosta foliage breaks down in winter, and deciduous trees provide natural mulch. "It's a little blanket for them," Marsha says. **left** 'Pandora's Box' is one of the all-time favorite hostas in American Hosta Society popularity polls. Marsha likes to mulch with pine needles to show off the hostas' color and form. **opposite** 'Stitch in Time' hosta offers wide, bright golden margins that contrast with narrow, dark green centers on leaves that reach about 6 inches long.

PINT-SIZE HOSTA HEAVEN

Miniature hostas are perfect as border plants or to fill in small spaces in a rock garden. We showcase some of our favorites in vintage McCoy planters to reveal their diminutive stature. Technically, not all of these are miniatures.

1. 'Radio Waves'
2. 'Pandora's Box'
3. 'Silver Threads and Golden Needles'
4. 'Blue Mouse Ears'
5. 'Cherish'
6. 'Dragon Tails'
7. 'Frosted Mouse Ears'
8. 'Kinbotan'
9. 'Chartreuse Wiggles'
10. 'Baby Bunting'
11. 'Dixie Chickadee'
12. 'Faithful Heart'
13. 'Mighty Mouse'
14. 'Little Jay'
15. 'Tears of Joy'
16. 'Holy Mouse Ears'
17. 'Cameo'
18. 'Corkscrew'
19. 'Cracker Crumbs'
20. 'Kinbotan'

Hostas pair well with lamium. Choose low-growing varieties when combining them in the front of a bed or as an edging plant along a pathway.

Little Charmers

MINI HOSTAS AT A GLANCE

The American Hosta Society classifies mini hostas (they prefer "mini" to "miniature") as plants with leaf blades no longer than 4½ inches and with an area no greater than about 4 square inches (about the size of a silver dollar). Mature plants (five years old) must not be taller than 6 inches.

You don't need a shovel to plant tiny hostas—a trowel will do. Plant them in well-drained soil enriched with compost in a shady spot. (In pots, mix a little compost with the potting soil.) Plant crowns should be at soil level. Mulch around mini hostas to conserve moisture, limit weeds, and show off the plants.

Generally, yellow-leaf hostas are the most sun-tolerant; hostas with white centers also need some sunlight. At Flying Frog Farms, Marsha Ansevics gives her hostas a balanced granular fertilizer once a month in summer. Fertilizer might burn hosta foliage, she says, so water well after applying it to knock the fertilizer off the leaves. She also feeds hostas with a water-soluble fertilizer once a month from May through August.

Keep an eye on young plants, especially the first year when they might need a little extra watering. "If they seem to be going downhill, move them," Marsha says. Mini hostas are also susceptible to frost heaving in spring; a rock or a brick tucked near the crown of each plant should help to prevent heaving.

Hostas are hardy in Zones 3–9.

opposite Hosta 'Heavenly Tiara' produces thick foliage that is light green at the center with a margin that changes from yellow to creamy white during the growing season. **above right** Hosta 'Pathfinder' boasts a white center with green sprinkles and a dark green margin on leaves that can reach 6 inches long. **right** 'Blue Mouse Ears' grows next to a leafy foamflower (tiarella) at the edge of a bed. The rounded, lightly cupped, bluish-green foliage is attractive in containers or as a low border plant. It reaches 8 inches tall at maturity.

CHAPTER SIX

Shade Plants Encyclopedia

Discover colorful options for shaded landscapes. Take your pick from perennials, annuals, groundcovers, shrubs, and trees.

YOU
— SHOULD KNOW —
Astilbe needs consistently moist soil to thrive. It's a good choice for areas that don't drain well.

Astilbe
Astilbe

Zones: **4–8**
Light: **Partial Sun, Shade**
Height: **Under 6 inches to 8 feet**
Width: **18–30 inches**
Color: **Blue, Pink, Red, White**
Bloom Time: **Spring, Summer**
Special Features: **Deer Resistant, Attracts Birds, Cut Flowers, Fragrance, Good for Containers**

Astilbe brings a graceful, feathering note to moist, shady landscapes. In cooler climates in the northern third or so of the U.S., it can tolerate full sun provided it has a constant supply of moisture. In drier sites, however, the leaves will scorch in full sun.

Feathery plumes of white, pink, lavender, or red flowers rise above finely divided foliage from early to late summer depending on the variety. It will spread slowly over time where well-situated. Most commercially available types are complex hybrids. 'Deutschland' astilbe bears pure white flowers and is a stunning addition to an all-white border. 'Fanal' offers dark red plumes and bronzy foliage.

Planting Companions

Hosta The round or almond-shape leaves of hosta add sharp contrast to the spiky flower plumes of astilbe.

Coralbells Soft mounds of heuchera foliage add colorful contrast when paired with astilbe.

Japanese painted fern Lacy, colorful fronds of Japanese painted fern add contrast and texture to shaded gardens.

VARIETIES

1. 'SPRITE' won the Perennial Plant of the Year Award in 1994. Its airy light pink flower panicles are highly branched and appear over glossy green-toothed foliage.

2. 'OSTRICH PLUME' offers large weeping pink flower clusters that bring elegance to the woodland border. The 30- to 36-inch-tall panicles form in late spring to early summer.

Bigroot Geranium
Geranium macrorrhizum

Zones: **3–8**

Light: **Shade, Partial Shade, Sun**

Height: **12–18 inches**

Width: **18–24 inches**

Color: **Pink, White**

Bloom Time: **Mid-Spring, Late Summer**

Special Features: **Good in Containers, Deer Resistant, Rabbit Resistant, Long Blooming**

Also called cranesbill geranium, this is one of the toughest plants for the shade garden. Bigroot geranium doesn't mind heat or drought. It makes a fine groundcover and tolerates dry, light shade. Deer and rabbits typically pass it by in search of tastier morsels. This shade plant puts on a spring show with pink, magenta, or white flowers; some varieties also offer red and bronze foliage in autumn. This perennial has an attractive mounding habit. Plants flower for a month or more, so it's a colorful asset to the shade garden. When plants stop blooming, shear off spent blooms to encourage another flush of flowering. Because this perennial geranium thrives in both sun and shade, it is an especially useful plant in yards that receive multiple types of light.

Planting Companions

Toad lily Add height and interest to your shade garden by planting bigroot geranium in front of toad lilies.

Hosta The fine foliage of bigroot geranium contrasts nicely with large-leaf hosta varieties. The colorful flowers of the geranium brighten marginal areas that receive both sun and shade.

Lamium A lower-growing groundcover than bigroot geranium, lamium provides variegated foliage and soft pink flowers.

YOU
— SHOULD KNOW —
Bigroot geranium is drought tolerant and a good choice for water-wise landscaping. It also self-sows freely.

VARIETIES

1. 'INGWERSEN'S VARIETY' bears light pink flowers with dark sepals held high above dark green foliage. It grows 12–18 inches tall and spreads 15 inches wide. It makes an ideal groundcover. Zones 4–8

2. GERANIUM MACRORRHIZUM is a lush and colorful groundcover. Try 'Bevan's Variety', which bears rose/red flowers, and 'Album' for white flowers. Zones 3–8

YOU
SHOULD KNOW
By midsummer, old-fashioned bleeding heart usually goes dormant and loses its foliage.

Bleeding Heart, Old Fashioned
Dicentra spectabilis

Zones: **3–9**
Light: **Shade, Partial Sun**
Height: **4 feet**
Width: **1–3 feet**
Color: **Pink, White**
Bloom Time: **Spring**
Special Features: **Deer Resistant, Good for Containers, Cut Flowers, Low Maintenance**

It's easy to see the origin of bleeding heart's common name when you get a look at its heart-shape pink or white blooms with a protruding tip at the base of the heart. And there's little wonder why old-fashioned bleeding heart is a favorite of plants that grow in shade. In late spring and early summer, it produces gorgeous flowers that hang from elegant arching stems. Bleeding heart blooms are elegant additions to bouquets where their arching stems of heart-shape flowers can be viewed at close perspective. To grow bleeding heart, plant in partial to full shade in moist, well-drained soil.

Planting Companions

Hosta In early spring, hostas rise from the ground, unfolding lovely rounded leaves that contrast nicely with bleeding heart's fine-cut foliage.

Virginia bluebells Blooming at the same time as old-fashioned bleeding heart, Virginia bluebells feature clusters of bell-shape blooms that look stunning with pink and white bleeding heart.

Spring-flowering bulbs Bleeding heart is lovely paired with small early-spring-blooming bulbs such as blue scilla and yellow miniature daffodils.

VARIETIES

1. 'GOLD HEART' This bleeding heart offers a dramatic color combination for spring gardens. It pairs showy chartreuse foliage with pink blooms.

2. 'ALBA' White flowering bleeding hearts offer the same gorgeous flower shape in snow white. White bleeding hearts are beautiful additions to all-white borders; they bloom in early spring.

Blue Fescue
Festuca glauca

Zones: **4–8**
Light: **Partial Sun, Sun**
Height: **6–10 inches**
Width: **6–10 inches**
Color: **White Flowers; Blue Foliage**
Bloom Time: **Spring through Fall**
Special Features: **Attracts Birds, Good for Containers, Low Maintenance**

One of the most versatile ornamental grasses, blue fescue can be used in many different ways. Plant it at the base of leggy shrubs or tall perennials, such as lilies, to help them blend with the landscape and offset the other plant flowers or foliage. Plant in masses as a groundcover or in rows as an edging plant. Use as an accent in a rock garden or flower border. It even looks fabulous in containers.

Blue fescue is evergreen in all but its northernmost range. The fine bluish foliage looks best when it is fresh in spring and early summer. Seed heads turn tan when mature. You may want to cut them off to keep plants tidy.

Planting Companions

Dianthus The blue-green foliage of dianthus closely matches that of fescue. Top it off with pink blooms and you have a dramatic combination.

Blanketflower Mounds of gold, orange, and maroon daisies of blanketflower team superbly with spiky bluish mounds of blue fescue foliage.

Shrub rose Blue fescue makes an attractive groundcover at the base of a rose bush.

YOU SHOULD KNOW
Blue fescue produces seed heads that turn tan when mature. To keep plants tidy, clip them off.

VARIETIES

1. 'ELIJAH BLUE' forms a compact 8- to 10-inch-tall tuft of fine bluish-green leaves.

2. 'SEA URCHIN' is also sometimes listed by its official name 'Seeigel'. It forms a dense 10-inch-tall mound.

Corydalis
Corydalis lutea

Zones: **5–8**
Light: **Partial Shade, Full Shade**
Height: **12–18 inches**
Width: **12–18 inches**
Color: **Yellow**
Bloom Time: **Late Spring through Autumn**
Special Features: **Deer Resistant, Good for Containers**

This hardworking, shade-loving beauty takes the prize for being the longest bloomer in the sheltered garden. This woodland perennial forms a beautiful mound of ferny leaves topped with clusters of yellow flowers from late spring all the way to frost. Flowers resemble those of bleeding heart.

Use corydalis in rock gardens or as edging plants in the front of borders. This perennial naturalizes well, meaning that it will spread. When growing in optimum conditions, it may self-seed readily. Corydalis prefers moist soil with good drainage. There are several types of corydalis. *Corydalis lutea* is the easiest to grow and the longest blooming. White corydalis (*Corydalis ochroleuca*) flowers over an extended period.

Planting Companions

Japanese maple The finely cut, colorful leaves of Japanese maple are a beautiful companion with the footlight effect of yellow corydalis planted beneath.

Solomon's seal The arching stems and dangling creamy bell-like flowers of this perennial contrast well with corydalis, which is shorter and more compact.

Barrenwort This perennial spreads like groundcover and produces small flowers shaped like a bishop's miter (which is how it got its common name of bishop's cap).

VARIETIES

1. BLUE PANDA This blue *Corydalis flexuosa* bears elongated blue flowers with spurs; it blooms in spring.

2. BLACKBERRY WINE sports fragrant wine-purple tubular flowers from late spring through early summer, or longer in cool climates. It has elegant lacy leaves.

Doronicum
Doronicum orientale

Zones: **4–7**
Light: **Partial Sun, Shade**
Height: **6 inches to 4 feet**
Width: **12–15 inches**
Color: **Yellow, Gold**
Bloom Time: **Spring**
Special Features: **Good for Containers, Low Maintenance, Attracts Butterflies**

Doronicum, also commonly called leopard's bane and caucasian leopard's bane, produces bright yellow daisylike flowers that light up the shadiest areas. This easy-care, versatile perennial features varieties that range in edging types that grow just 6 inches tall to back-of-the-border beauties that reach 4 feet tall. Plants bear clusters of sunny flowers in spring, then die back once summer temperatures rise. The foliage is heart-shape. Plants grow in a nice mound or clump. Where suited to the climate, doronicum is easy to grow as long as it has rich, moist, well-drained soil. Deadhead plants after blooms fade to encourage repeat flowering in fall.

Planting Companions

Impatiens Reliable and colorful, impatiens adds bright beauty to shade all season long. This annual blooms in nearly every color except true blue and grows well as border edgers or in containers.

Narcissus Spring-flowering narcissus (also called daffodil) is the ideal companion for doronicum. Plant yellow and white narcissus to complement doronicum's sunny yellow flowers.

Astilbe The plume-like flowers of astilbe contrast well with doronicum's round daisylike flowers.

YOU
— SHOULD KNOW —
Mulching around the base of plants will help improve their hardiness in colder climates.

VARIETIES

1. 'LITTLE LEO' grows 10–14 inches tall and has semidouble yellow daisylike flowers in spring. Doronicum is a pollinator attractant and will draw bees and butterflies to garden beds or containers.

2. DORONICUM ORIENTALE produces daisylike flowers in bright yellow or gold. An early spring bloomer, doronicum may also rebloom when faded flowers are removed.

YOU SHOULD KNOW

Fill a pair of urns or other traditional containers with large ferns to create instant ambience.

Ferns

Many species

Zones: **2–10**
Light: **Shade, Partial Shade**
Height: **1–4 feet**
Width: **1–4 feet**
Color: **Green Foliage**
Bloom Time: **Leaves look good from spring through fall**
Special Features: **Good for Containers, Low Maintenance**

Graceful, lacy fronds add textural intrigue to landscapes and container plantings. Whether upright or arching, ferns are elegant companions to more colorful growers such as impatiens, begonia, and coleus. Use beautiful maidenhair ferns to add an airy, delicate texture in shade garden containers. Maidenhair ferns are lovely grouped in a shady, moist, well-drained location, forming a fine-textured mass. Ostrich ferns offer large showy leaves and are beautiful massed together. Lady fern is a woodland native that thrives in moist or wet soil. Although not as showy as ostrich fern, lady fern makes an ideal and dense groundcover.

Planting Companions

Hosta Flat or puckered large leaves of hosta provide dramatic contrast to the finely divided, frilly fronds of maidenhair fern or ostrich fern.

Begonia Pink, white, and red begonias add colorful highlights to dark green fern fronds.

Coleus Splashy coleus is a colorful companion for ferns. Use pink- and chartreuse-hue coleus to brighten fern-filled containers.

VARIETIES

1. OSTRICH FERN *Matteuccia struthiopteris* is popular for its erect stature and graceful arching fronds (leaves) that resemble huge ostrich feathers. It grows 1–4 feet tall. Zones 2–8

2. AMERICAN MAIDENHAIR FERN *Adiantum pedatum* is native to North America and bears upright black or brown stalks with featherlike medium-green fronds. It grows 12–16 inches tall. Zones 3–8

Fern-Leaf Bleeding Heart

Dicentra eximina and *Dicentra formosa*

Zones: **4–8**
Light: **Shade, Partial Shade**
Height: **2 feet**
Width: **1–3 feet**
Color: **Red, White, Pink**
Bloom Time: **Late Spring, Summer, Fall**
Special Features: **Long Blooming, Edging Plants, Good for Containers, Deer Resistant**

Fern-leaf bleeding heart looks beautiful all season. This shade lover has a neat, compact growth habit, and it blooms on and off from spring to fall (with enough moisture during hot, dry periods). The heart-shape flowers are borne in delicate clusters of pink, red, or white. Even when not in bloom, tidy mounds of blue-green, ferny foliage are stunning planted amid other shade-loving companions, especially with contrasting leaves. *Dicentra eximia* has deeply cut blue-green foliage and pink blooms rising to 1 foot tall. It reblooms through summer and fall as long as temperatures are not too hot. *Dicentra formosa*, also called Western bleeding heart, grows 6 inches to 1 foot tall and blooms in late spring. It is fairly drought tolerant in summer months.

Planting Companions

Yellow corydalis Create subtle contrast of two shade lovers that have finely cut foliage by pairing fern-leaf bleeding heart varieties with yellow corydalis.

Chartreuse or blue hosta The blue-green or blue-gray foliage of fern-leaf bleeding heart is stunning with varieties of light green or blue-hue hosta varieties.

YOU SHOULD KNOW
If you remove the faded flowers of fern-leaf bleeding heart, it will encourage the formation of new buds and flowers.

VARIETIES

1. 'KING OF HEARTS' offers rose-pink flowers that are borne above blue-green foliage. It grows 8–10 inches tall and spreads 12–16 inches wide. Zones 2–8

2. 'BURNING HEARTS' offers heart-shape rose-color flowers from late spring through summer (the cooler the summer, the longer the bloom). Foliage is blue-gray. It grows 8–12 inches tall and spreads 12–15 inches wide. Zones 5–9

Hairgrass
Deschampsia caespitosa

Zones: **4–9**
Light: **Shade, Partial Shade**
Height: **1–3 feet**
Width: **1–2 feet**
Color: **Green, Chartreuse, Gold Foliage**
Bloom Time: **Summer, Fall; Foliage looks good from spring through summer**
Special Features: **Colorful Fall Foliage, Cut Flowers, Good for Containers, Low Maintenance**

Tufted hairgrass gets its name from fine hairlike flowers that rise about the plant. They emerge green and turn shades of gold, forming clouds that look like a beautiful unruly head of golden hair. A native to damp woods, bogs, and streamsides, tufted hairgrass prefers a cool spot in partial shade.

Planting Companions

Ligularia appreciates moist soil, as does tufted hairgrass. Its coarse mound of foliage contrasts dramatically with airy clouds of tufted hairgrass blooms.

Primrose is ideal for adding brilliant color around the base of tufted hairgrass. It also appreciates partial shade and moist potting mix.

Iris features tall spiky foliage and flowers in a rainbow of colors. The rigid structure of iris is beautiful with the soft foliage of tufted hairgrass.

VARIETIES

1. 'TARDIFLORA' *Deschampsia cespitosa* 'Tardiflora' is a variegated hairgrass that blooms in late summer with greenish clouds of flowers over a mound of medium-green foliage. Zones 4–9

2. 'NORTHERN LIGHTS' *Deschampsia caespitosa* 'Northern Lights' is a green grass with creamy white variegation. Enjoy this nice touch: Leaves turn pink in cold weather. Zones 4–9

Hosta
Hosta selections

Zones: **3–9**
Light: **Shade, Partial Shade**
Height: **Up to 5 feet**
Width: **Up to 4 feet**
Color: **Green, White, Cream, Yellow, Blue Foliage; White, Lavender Flowers**
Bloom Time: **Summer**
Special Features: **Edging Plants, Good for Containers**

This leafy plant, which was rarely grown just 40 years ago, is now one of the most common shade garden plants. Hosta has earned its spot in the hearts of gardeners because it's among the easiest plants to grow, as long as your garden has some shade and ample rainfall. Hostas vary from tiny plants suitable for troughs or small containers to massive 4-foot clumps with heart-shape leaves that can fill large spaces in the garden, much like shrubs. The gorgeous foliage of hostas makes it a cherished and versatile shade plant; varieties feature a wide range of leaf structure: puckered, wavy-edged, white or green variegated, blue-gray, chartreuse, emerald-edged— variations are nearly endless.

Planting Companions

Astilbe and hosta are classic partners for shaded places. Astilbe's finely cut foliage and colorful flower plumes complement hosta's round and heart-shape leaves.

Holly fern The upright fronds of Christmas fern contrast well against the solid foliage of hosta in shade.

Columbine The dancing, colorful flowers of columbine bloom when hostas are beginning to unfurl young leaves.

YOU
— SHOULD KNOW —
Cut the long flowering stems of white or purplish flowers from hostas for bouquets.

VARIETIES

1. 'BLUE MOUSE EARS' This tiny hosta is a charming dwarf selection with rounded blue leaves. It grows 5 inches tall and 12 inches wide. Blue hostas add subtle color to foliage borders. Zones 3–9

2. 'AZTEC TREASURE' Brighten any shaded spot with 1-foot mounds of heart-shape chartreuse leaves and bell-shape purple flowers in summer. Zones 3–8

YOU SHOULD KNOW
Common names for hellebores are Christmas rose (because there are types that bloom in late winter) and Lenten rose (because there are types that bloom in late spring).

Hellebore
Helleborus

Zones: **4–9**
Light: **Shade, Partial Shade**
Height: **1–3 feet**
Width: **1–3 feet**
Color: **Burgundy, Pink, Cream, Green, White Flowers; Gold, Chartreuse Foliage**
Bloom Time: **Late Winter, Early Spring**
Special Features: **Deer Resistant, Rabbit Resistant**

Hellebores are so easy and so pretty, they have a place in nearly every landscape. Their exquisite bowl- or saucer-shape flowers in white (often speckled), pinks, yellows, or maroon remain on the plant for several months, even after the petals have fallen. Deer-resistant and mostly evergreen, hellebores' divided leaves rise on sturdy stems and may be serrated (like a knife) along the edges. Grow hellebores in shade where soil remains moist; some hellebores prefer acid or alkaline conditions, depending on variety.

Planting Companions

Gold-leaf coralbells such as 'Lime Rickey' or 'Citronelle' shine bright against dark green hellebore leaves.

Astilbe features feathery plumes of white, pink, lavender, or red flowers that rise above finely divided foliage from early to late summer, depending on the variety. These beauties can fill in around hellebores in the summer garden.

Lungwort Brilliant blue, pink, or white flowers of lungwort blooms appear in early spring for ideal partners with hellebores. The spotted or plain leaves are handsome throughout the season and into winter. Plant close as a weed-discouraging groundcover or in borders as edgings or bright accent plants.

VARIETIES

1. 'PINK FROST' helleborus features burgundy buds that open to a pale pink flower. Plants have dark red stems. Zones 5–8

2. HYBRID HELLEBORES A large number of hybrid strains have leathery evergreen leaves and nodding bowl-shape flowers (including doubles!) in an ever-expanding range of colors (except blue). Zones 6–9

Jacob's Ladder
Polemonium selections

Zones: **4–9**
Light: **Shade, Partial Shade**
Height: **1–3 feet**
Width: **6 inches to 2 feet**
Color: **White, Pink, Blue, Lavender, Yellow Flowers; Variegated Foliage**
Bloom Time: **Spring, Early Summer**
Special Features: **Cut Flowers, Good for Containers**

Jacob's ladder is a favorite native plant for shady or partially shady spots. (It will tolerate full sun when growing in cooler areas.) This plant produces handsome long leaves, sometimes variegated, with a ladderlike arrangement of leaflets. Plants produce heavy clusters of cup-shape flowers in a wide range of pastel colors: lavender-blue, pink, yellow, or white flowers with conspicuous stamens that nod atop slender stems. Jacob's ladder is a winner in lightly shaded areas; place containers on porches or patios that receive dappled light. Plants may reseed but are not invasive. As plants get taller, they may require staking. When plants complete bloom, cut back to encourage repeat flowering.

Planting Companions
Coralbells The dainty spires of red or pink coralbells are fine companions for Jacob's ladder in light shade. Create colorful combinations in containers.

Phlox Creeping phlox has flattish flowers in pinks, blues, and white that mix well with those of blue Jacob's ladder in light shade. Use creeping phlox at the front of a border with Jacob's ladder behind.

Candytuft The dark leaves and dramatic white flower heads of perennial candytuft provides a strong foil for Jacob's ladder in cool, sunny spots.

YOU SHOULD KNOW Mulch during winter in cooler climates. Jacob's ladder is susceptible to mildew. There are white Album and variegated cultivars

VARIETIES
1. 'STAIRWAY TO HEAVEN' *Polemonium reptans* 'Stairway to Heaven' bears pink-and-white-edged leaves and lavender-blue flowers in early summer. It grows 2 feet tall. Zones 3–7

2. 'BRIZE D'ANJOU' *Polemonium caeruleum* 'Brize D'Anjou' is not as floriferous as many others, but its leaves are dramatically rimmed with creamy white. It grows 2 feet tall. Zones 4–9

YOU SHOULD KNOW

Heucheras don't like soggy soil. Make sure they are planted in garden beds and containers in soil that drains well.

Heuchera

Heuchera selections

Zones: **3–9**
Light: **Partial Sun, Shade**
Height: **2–3 feet**
Width: **6–30 inches**
Color: **Pink, Red, White Flowers; Russet, Bronze, Green, Chartreuse Foliage**
Bloom Time: **Summer; foliage looks beautiful from spring through fall**
Special Features: **Good in Containers, Low Maintenance**

Exciting new selections with incredible foliage patterns have put heucheras, also called coralbells, on the map. Previously enjoyed mainly for spires of dainty reddish flowers, coralbells are now grown as much for the unusual mottling and veining of different-color leaves. Low clumps of long-stem evergreen or semi-evergreen lobed foliage make coralbells beautiful container plants. They enjoy humus-rich, moisture-retaining soil. Beware of heaving in areas with very cold winters.

Planting Companions

Astilbe The fluffy red, pink, or white flower plumes and ferny leaves of astilbe combine well with coralbells in shaded, moist sites.

Hosta Bold-foliage hostas that prefer moist soil and somewhat shaded conditions are perfect partners for coralbells.

Japanese painted fern Delicately variegated markings of Japanese painted fern echo the markings on coralbells.

VARIETIES

1. 'DOLCE BLACKCURRANT' offers rich purple leaves with splashes of silver. It grows 16 inches tall and 20 inches wide. Zones 4–9

2. 'DOLCE KEY LIME PIE' features exciting lime green foliage from spring to fall and clusters of pink flowers in spring. It grows 16 inches tall and 14 inches wide. Zones 4–9

Japanese Forestgrass

Hakonechloa macra

Zones: **5–9**
Light: **Partial Sun, Shade**
Height: **1–3 feet**
Width: **12–16 inches**
Color: **Green, Chartreuse Foliage**
Bloom Time: **Not Applicable**
Special Features: **Deer Resistant, Drought Tolerant, Slope Control, Good for Containers**

Also called hakone grass, Japanese forestgrass offers color and texture for the shade garden. The elegant, sweeping lines of this grass are so lovely that it's a favorite among gardeners. And Japanese forestgrass is one of only a few ornamental grasses that thrive in shade. Its mounding clumps of arching grassy leaves gradually increase in size over time, but it never becomes invasive. Use hakone grass along garden edges in woodland gardens or in containers on shaded porches or patios. Variegated cultivars are particularly attractive because they brighten dark spots. All types of this perennial grass thrive in moisture-retaining, humus-rich soil and even tolerate dry conditions.

Planting Companions

Golden hosta Add zing to a shady corner by planting Japanese forestgrass with a bold golden hosta. Variegated hakone grass contrasts well with large-leaf chartreuse varieties of hosta.

Columbine These tall cottage-garden favorites produce flowers in almost every color. They add spots of color behind hakone grass in a border or bed.

Holly fern has evergreen fronds that always look good and mixes well with Japanese forestgrass.

YOU
— SHOULD KNOW —
This beautiful grass is lovely in the landscape but also excels in containers. Combine it with other shade lovers, such as begonias, or plant it alone in large containers.

VARIETIES

1. **'AUREOLA'** is an ideal option for brightening gently shaded places. Its lovely golden-yellow leaves are striped with green and arch gracefully toward the light.

2. **'ALL GOLD'** features bright golden foliage that grows in an attractive clump. This perennial grass add brilliant yellow tones to a shaded spot. In dense shade, the color will be more chartreuse.

YOU
— **SHOULD KNOW** —
The silvery foliage of Japanese painted fern achieves its best color when it gets a few hours of morning sunshine.

Japanese Painted Fern
Athyrium niponicum var. *pictum*

Zones: **4–9**
Light: **Partial Sun, Shade**
Height: **1–3 feet**
Width: **1–2 feet**
Color: **Gray, Silver, Purple, Burgundy**
Bloom Time: **Not Applicable**
Special Features: **Good in Containers, Low Maintenance, Deer Resistant, Rabbit Resistant**

One of the most elegant ferns available for gardens, Japanese painted ferns are washed with gorgeous silver and burgundy markings. Plus, they're low-growing and slow-spreading. Unlike most ferns, these toughies will tolerate dry soil. And they will tolerate some sun if they have ample water. Lady fern is closely related to Japanese painted fern, and they are sometimes crossed with each other to create attractive hybrids.

Planting Companions

'Burgundy Glow' ajuga has silvery purple tones, which is a beautiful color companion with Japanese painted fern. It is a low-growing perennial that can sit at the feet of the taller fern.

Pink impatiens offers pops of color that pair beautifully with Japanese painted fern, especially those with silver-gray accents.

Lady's mantle is stunning planted near Japanese painted fern. Its scalloped leaves catch rain or dewdrops, making the foliage look as if it is studded with jewels.

VARIETIES

1. 'SILVER FALLS' has pinkish-red stems and reddish-purple veins. It is most colorful with a few hours of sun per day. Zones 5–8

2. 'BURGUNDY LACE' has dramatic purple leaves that are frosted with silvery accents. This fern is more tolerant of heat than other ferns. Zones 4–8

Lungwort
Pulmonaria

Zones: **2–8**
Light: **Shade, Partial Shade, Sun**
Height: **Under 6 inches**
Width: **1–2 feet**
Color: **Blue, Pink, White Flowers; White Mottled Foliage**
Bloom Time: **Spring, Summer**
Special Features: **Deer Resistant, Rabbit Resistant, Groundcover, Low Maintenance**

In early spring, brilliant blue, pink, or white flowers of lungwort bloom despite the coldest chill. The rough basal leaves, spotted or plain, are attractive and continue to be handsome throughout the season and into winter. Planted closely as a weed-discouraging groundcover or in borders as edgings or bright accent plants, lungworts are workhorses that retain good looks. Provide high-humus soil that retains moisture. Although lungwort tolerates dry conditions, be alert for mildew. Lungwort is one of the hardiest shade perennials, and plants will last for years, spreading and creating larger attractive clumps.

Planting Companions

Japanese painted fern is a pretty companion to lungwort because they both feature foliage flecked with white.

'Jack Frost' brunnera paired with silvery-foliage lungwort creates a delightful silver-on-silver play.

White impatiens offers pure-white petals that pick up the white dappling of lungwort leaves.

YOU
— SHOULD KNOW —
Because its foliage is somewhat hairy, deer and rabbits typically leave lungwort alone.

VARIETIES

1. 'OPAL' This beauty produces shell-pink buds that open to ice-blue blooms. The white-flecked foliage accents the white flowers. Grows 8 to 12 inches tall. Zones 3–8

2. 'SILVER SHIMMERS' is an excellent lungwort for foliage appeal. The silver-plated almond-shape leaves have freckles at the edges. This lungwort turns on the lights in dark spots. Zones 4–9

YOU
— SHOULD KNOW —
Monkshood, commonly called wolfsbane, is a poisonous plant. Keep out of reach from children and pets. When handling the plant, use garden gloves.

Monkshood

Aconitum

Zones: **3–8**
Light: **Partial Sun, Sun**
Height: **1–8 feet**
Width: **1 foot**
Color: **Blue, White, Purple**
Bloom Time: **Summer, Fall**
Special Features: **Deer Resistant, Rabbit Resistant**

How can you not fall in love with a perennial that has regal blue spires? Monkshood is that plant. Relatively unknown, it deserves a lot more attention. It produces tall spikes of hooded purple, blue, white, or bicolor blooms in late summer to fall. When not in bloom, its mounds of coarsely lobed foliage have garden interest. Plants grow best in partial shade, although in cool climates they will grow well in full sun. In dense shade, plants will become floppy. All parts of monkshood are poisonous. Monkshood does not tolerate hot weather and is not a good choice for hot-summer climates.

Planting Companions

Kirengeshoma is a beautiful, underused perennial with bold foliage and yellow flowers in late summer.

Astilbe brings a graceful, feathering note to moist, shady landscapes. In cooler climates in the northern third or so of the U.S., it can tolerate full sun provided it has a constant supply of moisture.

Toad lily is an Asian perennial that blooms with orchidlike flowers that demand a close look. It's an ideal choice for perennial gardens in need of fall color.

VARIETIES

1. BICOLOR features pale lavender to violet flowers with darker purple petals below. It grows 4 feet tall. Zones 3–7

2. ACONITUM NAPELLUS blooms in deep purple-blue in late summer. Plants grow to 5 feet tall. Zones 5–8

Oxalis
Oxalis selections

Zones: **6–11**
Light: **Part Sun, Shade**
Height: **12 inches**
Width: **12 inches**
Color: **White, Lavender, Yellow Flowers; Red, Purple, Green, Yellow Foliage**
Bloom Time: **Foliage looks good from spring through fall**
Special Features: **Low Maintenance, Groundcover**

Also known as shamrock plant and wood sorrel, oxalis features a trio of heart-shape green or purple leaves that may be marked with black or silver. This easy-to-grow charmer works both indoors and out. Oxalis bears colorful cloverlike leaves that fold up at night. They appear in a range of colors from silver to purple—and several are variegated with other colors. Cup-shape small blooms are dainty and attractive.

Planting Companions

Hosta Wavy heart-shape leaves of hosta make an excellent planting friend, especially to purple-leaf oxalis.

Sedum Pair a low-growing sedum, such as 'Dragon's Blood', with oxalis to create a colorful container for shady spots.

Daffodil Small spring-blooming daffodils look perky rising up from a bed of leafy oxalis.

YOU
— SHOULD KNOW —
Most oxalis selections do best in part to full shade and well-drained soil. Be sure not to overwater.

VARIETIES

1. 'MOLTEN LAVA' *Oxalis vulcanicola* 'Molten Lava' produces stunning orange-chartreuse foliage and decorative golden-yellow flowers all spring and summer. It grows 10 inches tall and wide. Zones 9–11, or try it as a houseplant.

2. 'IRON CROSS' *Oxalis tetraphylla* 'Iron Cross' has leaves divided into four leaflets. The center of each is decorated with a purple blotch that complements pink flowers. It grows 10 inches tall and wide. Zones 8–9, though it also thrives as a houseplant.

YOU
SHOULD KNOW
Prune alternanthera to keep the plant from taking over containers.

Alternanthera

Alternanthera selections

Light: **Partial Sun, Sun**
Height: **6–36 inches**
Width: **6–18 inches**
Color: **Red, Purple, Variegated Foliage**
Bloom Time: **Foliage looks good from spring through fall**
Special Features: **Good for Containers, Low Maintenance, Groundcover, Slope Control**

The two common names given to this tropical plant—calico plant or Joseph's coat—say it all: Its richly colorful leaves in purples, bronzes, oranges, reds, and yellows make it an exciting container candidate. In the tropics, it's a perennial, but most gardeners grow it as an annual. It's a top pick for containers, and if you have a sunny window, you can even take it inside as a houseplant. Like so many tropical plants, alternanthera likes rich, moist, well-drained potting mix.

Planting Companions

Angelonia has richly colorful upright flower spikes that pair well with variegated forms.

Dusty miller Go for high contrast by combining a deep purple-red variety of alternanthera with the silvery foliage of dusty miller.

Fountaingrass Complement dark-on-dark combination with an explosion of purple fountaingrass foliage bursting out from a carpet of alternanthera.

VARIETIES

1. JOSEPH'S COAT bears purplish foliage on a spreading low plant perfect for containers and window boxes.

2. 'GAIL'S CHOICE' offers dark purple-red foliage on an upright plant that can reach 3 feet tall.

Asparagus Fern
Asparagus selections

Light: **Partial Shade, Sun**

Height: **18–36 inches**

Width: **18–36 inches**

Color: **White**

Bloom Time: **Foliage looks good from spring through fall; when mature, produces red berries**

Special Features: **Low Maintenance, Good for Containers**

This subtropical relative of edible garden asparagus is in the lily family, but its needlelike foliage resembles a fern. As its stems shoot up and outward, it is an excellent plant for hanging baskets. Give asparagus fern medium to bright indoor light, and keep the soil uniformly moist. Plants sometimes develop small red berries, which are poisonous, so keep the berries away from children and pets.

Planting Companions

Blue lobelia Asparagus ferns offer a frilly cascade of green that complements the neon-blue flowers of lobelia.

Sweet alyssum Pair asparagus fern with lacy white sweet alyssum. As the fern spills over the container's side, sweet alyssum creates a frothy edge.

Geranium Pink or red geraniums are traditional companions with asparagus ferns.

YOU
— SHOULD KNOW —
Trim off old stems to encourage new growth and to keep asparagus ferns fresh and dense.

VARIETIES

1. **'MYERS'** has dense bottlebrush-like stems that grow more upright. It makes a better tabletop plant than hanging basket.

2. **'SPRENGERI'** is the most widely available variety; it has arching stems with 1-inch-long dark green needles.

YOU
— SHOULD KNOW —
Tuberous begonias are extremely sensitive to frost. Cover them or take them indoors when temperatures dip.

Begonia (tuberous)

Begonia × tuberhybrida

Light: **Shade, Partial Sun**
Height: **6–18 inches**
Width: **6–12 inches**
Color: **White, Pink, Red**
Bloom Time: **Summer through fall**
Special Features: **Good for Containers, Perennial in Zones 10–11**

Beautiful tuberous begonias are among the most elegant of shade-loving plants. These tender bulbs prefer humid, cool-summer climates. In these regions, intense colors brighten shady gardens as no other plant can. Big, bold blooms may be single or double as plants produce separate male and female flowers. Larger flowers on the plant are male and can reach 6 inches across. Many tuberous begonias have an arching plant habit, which makes them excellent for growing in hanging baskets or container gardens. In areas where they're not hardy, dig up the tubers before the first fall frost and store them dormant in a cool (35–40°F) place over winter. Start them indoors several weeks before the last frost date in your Zone. Begonias thrive on fertilizer, so be generous. No need to deadhead this flower unless you want to; it's "self-cleaning"!

Planting Companions

Impatiens Combining white begonias with any color of impatiens is a surefire way to create a colorful display in a shady spot.

Blue lobelia Give white begonias a colorful skirt of blue lobelia for a stunning mix.

Wishbone flower Combine wishbone flowers, with similar shape to begonias, for an intriguing, subtle container display.

VARIETIES

1. 'BELLAGIO APRICOT' is a double-flowering begonia for shade with pendulous apricot flowers ideal for hanging baskets. It grows 14 inches tall and 2 feet wide.

2. 'BONFIRE' offers glowing orange flowers and narrow bronzy-green leaves. It's especially effective in containers. It grows 20 inches tall and wide.

Begonia (fibrous)

Begonia semperflorens

Light: **Bright Shade, Sun**
Height: **18 inches**
Width: **18 inches**
Color: **Red, White, Pink**
Bloom Time: **Summer through fall**
Special Features: **Ideal for Bedding, Good for Containers and Window Boxes**

Also called wax begonia, this popular bedding plant provides swaths of rich color to shaded spots. Tucked into pots, wax begonias also add pops of color to mixed containers. Also grow wax begonia indoors, where it will bloom all year with enough light and good air movement. Simply take cuttings of plants in the garden for your indoor garden. Cuttings root quickly in water or moist potting soil. Make sure wax begonia has good air circulation, otherwise it may be attacked by fungal diseases. It's an easy bloomer with waxy foliage and colorful red, white, or pink flowers.

Planting Companions

Angelonia Tall flower-filled spikes of angelonia contrast nicely with the mounding effect of wax begonias.

Impatiens Combine wax begonias with impatiens in containers and window boxes. Both love shade, and they bloom in similar colors.

Variegated hosta Add white wax begonias to containers with variegated hostas. White begonia flowers will pick up the light in the leaves, making a pleasing pairing.

YOU
— SHOULD KNOW —
Wax begonias come in varieties with green or bronze foliage. Mix and match them for beautiful planters and window boxes.

VARIETIES

1. 'YANG PINK' Soft pink flowers contrast nicely with green leaves. This begonia is very heat tolerant and offers rich color all season.

2. 'SPIRIT WHITE' Snow-white petals and bright green leaves make this a gorgeous choice for shaded beds and borders as well as containers.

YOU
— SHOULD KNOW —
In extreme heat, make sure to water nierembergia well. It doesn't tolerate dryness.

Cupflower
Nierembergia selections

Light: **Partial Shade**
Height: **1 foot**
Width: **2 feet**
Color: **White, Blue**
Bloom Time: **Summer through Fall**
Special Features: **Attracts Birds, Good for Containers, Low Maintenance, Perennial in Zones 7–10**

Although cupflower can grow in full sun, in hotter climates it does best with a little shade. The adorable cup-shape flowers of nierembergia and its neat growth habit make it a useful annual flower for containers. Plant a row along the front edge of a planter or window box for a crisp look (especially the white-flower varieties). As a medium-height plant, it visually ties together taller plants and cascading plants.

Planting Companions

Sweet alyssum Pair blue nierembergia with white sweet alyssum in containers for a colorful mound of flowers.

Flowering tobacco White-flowering varieties of flowering tobacco partner well with nierembergia's mounding habit and charming blooms.

Nigella Mix nierembergia's cup-shape flowers with lacy multipetal flowers of nigella for a long-blooming, charming combo.

VARIETIES

1. **'AUGUSTA BLUE SKIES'** is wonderfully heat- and drought-tolerant with lavender-blue flowers all summer long. It grows 12 inches tall and 24 inches wide.

2. **'MONT BLANC'** is an award-winning variety with pure white flowers on an 8-inch-tall plant.

Coleus
Solenostemon hybrids

Light: **Shade, Partial Shade, Sun (depending on variety)**
Height: **1–4 feet**
Width: **1–3 feet**
Color: **Red, Green, White, Burgundy, Pink Foliage; White Flowers**
Bloom Time: **Foliage looks good from spring through fall**
Special Features: **Good for Containers, Low Maintenance, Perennial in Zones 10–11**

YOU _ SHOULD KNOW _ Pinch the flower/bloom shoots of young coleus plants to make the plants produce bushier growth.

Add excitement to dim areas of your yard with shade- and sun-loving coleus varieties. Amazing arrays of color combinations and leaf textures are available. Choose from plants with scalloped, toothed, or fringed leaf edges. Trailing shade-loving coleus is an easy-to-grow annual foliage plant that adapts well to hanging baskets and container gardens where sprawling stems can drape over the edge of the planter. Coleus grows well even in the darkest corners if you give it water and a little fertilizer, and wait to site containers outdoors until after the weather is consistently warm. It will grow vigorously all summer; at the end of the season, take cuttings of coleus plants to grow over winter. Root in water or use rooting hormone and plant in potting soil.

Planting Companions
Solid-color coleus Solid-hue leaves mix well with multicolor coleus varieties.

Begonia Shade-loving begonias in ruby red mix well with complementary-color coleus. Both love shaded locations.

Hosta Large heart-shape leaves of hosta contrast nicely with coleus' splashy, colorful personality.

VARIETIES

1. 'TELLTALE HEART' has heart-shape leaves with scalloped green edges and a deep purple-maroon center. It is slow to flower, so it needs little pinching or pruning to maintain its trailing shape. It trails to 18 inches.

2. 'ATLAS' is a stocky shade-tolerant foliage plant with purplish maroon leaves splashed with contrasting bright green center. Bright green repeats in a narrow band edging each leaf. It grows 2 feet tall.

YOU
— SHOULD KNOW —
In large containers, use dicondra as a creeping groundcover; pair with trees, shrubs, or standard roses.

Dichondra
Dichondra argentea

Light: **Shade, Partial Sun, Sun**
Height: **2–6 inches**
Width: **3–6 feet**
Color: **Silver Foliage**
Bloom Time: **Foliage looks good from spring through fall**
Special Features: **Deer Resistant, Drought Resistant, Groundcover, Good for Containers, Low Maintenance, Perennial in Zones 10–11**

This striking trailing annual is a fresh new way to work elegant silver foliage into containers and other plantings. Native to areas of the Southwest, it's very heat- and drought-tolerant and prefers slightly dry soil. Count on it to look good all season long, even if it wilts a few times. A perennial in the very warmest parts of the U.S., dichondra is treated like an annual elsewhere. It needs well-drained soil (another reason to plant in containers); be careful to avoid wet spots if planted in the ground. Dichondra's strands of soft, small fan-shape leaves create a shimmering cascade from hanging baskets and containers.

Planting Companions

Ornamental pepper Create bold contrast by planting purple-leaf peppers with 'Silver Falls' dichondra.

Sage For an all-silver display, combine silver sage and dichondra. Both plants are quite heat- and drought-tolerant.

Verbena Dichondra looks stunning paired with red or pink flowers of verbena or other bloomers.

VARIETIES

1. 'SILVER FALLS' This striking new trailing annual is a fresh way to include elegant silver foliage in containers and other plantings. Perfect in a hanging basket, window box, or other container, this plant can trail up to 6 feet with showy, soft foliage.

2. 'EMERALD FALLS' 'Emerald Falls' offers deep green leaves and dense, symmetrical habit. The plant is very full and maintains a trim appearance.

English Ivy
Hedera helix

Light: **Partial Shade, Sun**
Height: **Climbs to 30 feet**
Width: **8–12 inches**
Color: **Green, Variegated Foliage**
Bloom Time: **Foliage looks good all year**
Special Features: **Perennial in Zones 5-9, Annual in Containers and Window Boxes**

Ivy has been used for ages as a shade-loving groundcover or vine; it creates a dense mat on the ground until it finds something to climb on, then sends aerial roots into its support to grow up. Because it has aerial roots, it's not the best choice for growing up brick walls. A woody-stem groundcover, English ivy trails gracefully over the edge of containers. Use the versatile vine to decorate a trellis or obelisk in a pot. Its lobed leaves may be solid green or variegated with white-and-green or green-and-yellow markings. Best grown in sun or partial shade, ivy eventually crowds out small, less-aggressive plants, so choose its companions wisely.

Planting Companions

Eugenia Plant English ivy as a great groundcover for formally clipped topiaries, such as eugenia or rosemary.

Begonia Plant with red, white, or pink begonias. Ivy is a vigorous filler for a window box.

Impatiens Interplant ivy with impatiens, a shade-tolerant annual. Ivy provides evergreen foliage all winter.

YOU — SHOULD KNOW —
Leave English ivy in window boxes all year. It tolerates cold to Zone 5 and provides green holiday decor.

VARIETIES

1. 'GLACIER' has bluish-green leaves washed with gray-green and white.

2. 'NEEDLEPOINT' has medium green leaves with a long, narrow central lobe. Its deeply lobed leaves give the plant fine texture.

YOU
– SHOULD KNOW –

Euphorbia 'Diamond Frost' can be brought indoors and used as a lacy foil to accent other houseplants.

Euphorbia
Euphorbia selections

Light: **Partial Sun, Sun**
Height: **3 feet**
Width: **2 feet**
Color: **White, Variegated Foliage; White Flowers**
Bloom Time: **Foliage looks good in spring, summer, and fall**
Special Features: **Deer Resistant, Drought Resistant, Good for Containers, Low Maintenance,**

If you'd like a low-maintenance annual for containers (or beds and borders), it's tough to find a better performer than euphorbia. This group of plants offers outstanding heat and drought resistance. Plus, they have a white milky sap that animals don't like, so they're rarely nibbled on by deer, rabbits, or other critters. (Be warned, though: The sap can irritate sensitive skin.) The wide variety of euphorbia selections offers varying heights, colors, and textures.

Planting Companions

Angelonia Angelonia's purple, white, or pink flowers are nice accents to 'Diamond Frost' euphorbia's frothy white flowers.

Coralbells Purple, bronze, or chartreuse coralbells make a beautiful textural contrast to 'Helena's Blush'.

Cosmos, especially white selections, are striking with a planting of snow on the mountain.

VARIETIES

1. 'DIAMOND FROST' is one of the most popular container plants. A wonderfully heat- and drought-tolerant plant, it produces a continuous supply of frothy blooms from spring to fall. It grows 18 inches tall and 24 inches wide.

2. SNOW ON THE MOUNTAIN *Euphorbia marginata* has green foliage that develops a white edge in late summer. This self-seeding annual bears clusters of white flowers. It grows 3 feet tall and 1 foot wide.

Fuchsia
Fuchsia selections

Light: **Shade, Partial Sun, Sun**
Height: **1–8 feet**
Width: **1–5 feet**
Color: **Pink, Red, White, Fuchsia, Orange**
Bloom Time: **Summer through Fall**
Special Features: **Attracts Birds, Good for Containers**

Exotic fuchsia is a fascinating flower, with lovely hanging lanternlike flowers in magentas, pinks, purples, and whites. If you're lucky, your fuchsia will attract hummingbirds. There are several types of fuchsia on the market. The most familiar to many gardeners are those grown in hanging baskets in the North. Recently, plant breeders have released a series of upright fuchsias with smaller flowers, often in tones of orange and red. Fuchsias are actually tender perennials grown as annuals outside tropical regions. Place them outside in spring after all danger of frost has passed. They need rich, well-drained soil and ample moisture.

Planting Companions

Browallia Complement hanging fuchsia with the star-shape blue flowers of browallia.

Dichondra The bright foliage of 'Silver Falls' dichondra will set off fuchsia, especially a dark-flowering type.

Impatiens White impatiens are stunning with any fuchsia, and a white-on-white combination is especially lovely in evening hours.

YOU _SHOULD KNOW_
Fuchsias do best in areas with cool summers; they fade in high heat, humidity, or drought.

VARIETIES

1. 'BLACK PRINCE' is a compact, upright variety that bears dark violet-and-red single flowers all summer long. It offers good heat tolerance and grows 2 feet tall and wide. Zones 8–10

2. 'DARK EYES' bears purple double flowers with cerise-red sepals on a plant that trails 2 feet and grows 30 inches wide. It tolerates heat well. Zones 8–10

**YOU
_ SHOULD KNOW _**
Impatiens wilt rapidly in hot weather; frequent watering is a must.

Impatiens
Impatiens selections

Light: **Shade**
Height: **1–3 feet**
Width: **1–2 feet**
Color: **White, Pink, Fuchsia, Orange, Yellow Flowers; Chartreuse/Gold Foliage**
Bloom Time: **Summer through Fall**
Special Features: **Groundcover, Good for Containers, Low Maintenance**

What would we do without impatiens? It's the old reliable for shade gardens when you want eye-popping color all season long. The plants bloom in just about every color except true blue and are well suited to growing in containers or in the ground. Impatiens look stunning bedded out, creating wide swaths of consistent color. Or you can mix colors to make a tableau of bright hues. If you have a bright spot indoors, you may be able to grow impatiens all year as an indoor plant.

Planting Companions
Browallia Mix blue browallia with pink, white, or lavender impatiens for a steady show of soft color all the way to fall.

Begonia Big, beautiful tuberous begonias are graceful accents to impatiens, especially double-flowering impatiens.

Wishbone flower Create subtle textural contrast by mixing wishbone flowers with impatiens plantings.

VARIETIES
1. **'SUPER ELFIN WHITE'** produces pure-white flowers on compact, 10-inch-tall plants.

2. **'FUSION INFRARED APRICOT'** bears apricot-pink flowers with yellow-orange throats. It grows 16 inches tall.

Lobelia
Lobelia selections

Light: **Shade, Partial Shade, Sun**
Height: **6 inches to 1 foot**
Width: **1 foot**
Color: **Blue, White, Pink**
Bloom Time: **Spring, Fall**
Special Features: **Groundcover, Erosion Control, Low Maintenance, Good for Containers**

There are few blues more intense and gorgeous than those found on annual lobelia. The mounding type, called edging lobelia, is beautiful for planting in rows, containers, and window boxes. The cascading type is stunning, like a sapphire waterfall spilling over the sides of pots. Annual lobelia is in its glory during the cool weather of spring and fall. Except for cool-summer areas, such as the Pacific Northwest or high altitudes, lobelia stops flowering during the heat of summer.

Planting Companions

Creeping Jenny Mix blue lobelia with golden creeping Jenny for a bright, contrasting display that spills from a container or hanging basket.

Dianthus Accent blue lobelia's beautiful flowers with bright-color dianthus (and enjoy the scent from dianthus, too).

Pansy Grow blue lobelia as an edging plant in containers with blue, purple, or white pansies.

YOU
— SHOULD KNOW —
After it blooms in spring, shear back lobelia and it will likely rebloom in fall.

VARIETIES

1. 'RIVIERA MIDNIGHT BLUE' bears dark blue flowers and bronze-tinged foliage on vigorous, mounding plants.

2. 'LUCIA DARK BLUE' offers gorgeous true-blue flowers on a trailing plant that's more heat-tolerant than many older varieties. It trails to 24 inches.

YOU
_ SHOULD KNOW _
Keep soil moist and fertilize lightly and regularly to keep New Guinea impatiens producing flowers.

New Guinea Impatiens
Impatiens selections

Light: **Partial Shade, Sun**
Height: **1–3 feet**
Width: **1–2 feet**
Color: **Orange, White, Pink, Red, Coral, Bicolor Flowers; Chartreuse/Gold, Purple/Burgundy Foliage**
Bloom Time: **Summer, Fall**
Special Features: **Good for Containers, Low Maintenance**

Like its more common cousin, New Guinea impatiens provides hard-to-find brilliant color in shade. And it's not just the flowers. The foliage is often brilliantly, exotically colorful as well. These tropical plants really shine in containers, where they thrive in the perfect soil and drainage. They also do well in the ground as long as you take time to improve the soil and work in plenty of compost. They're a bit more sun-tolerant than common impatiens. Plant established New Guinea impatiens in spring after all danger of frost has passed.

Planting Companions

Dianthus Grow low varieties of dianthus with New Guinea impatiens for a colorful display all season.

Impatiens While New Guinea impatiens tolerates sun, it also does fine in shade. Create a fun mix by planting New Guinea impatiens with mini impatiens.

Sweet potato vine In containers, dress up dark-leaf New Guinea impatiens with the bright foliage of chartreuse sweet potato vine.

VARIETIES

1. 'APPLAUSE ORANGE BLAZE' bears bright orange flowers over variegated foliage. It's more cold-tolerant than many other varieties and grows 1 foot tall and wide.

2. 'CELEBRETTE DEEP RED' produces rich red flowers, which attract hummingbirds, over dark green foliage. It grows 10 inches tall.

Pansy
Viola selections

Light: **Partial Sun, Sun**
Height: **Under 6 inches to 3 feet**
Width: **4–12 inches**
Color: **Blue, Violet, Purple, White, Yellow, Cream, Orange**
Bloom Time: **Spring, Fall**
Special Features: **Good for Containers, Fragrant, Perennials in Zones 2–11**

From tiny cheerful Johnny jump-ups to stunning 3-inch blooms of Majestic Giant pansies, the genus *Viola* has a spectacular array of delightful plants for the spring garden. They're must-haves to celebrate the first days of spring, since they don't mind cold weather and can even take a little snow and ice! They're cherished for the early color they bring to pots, window boxes, and other containers. By summer, pansies bloom less and foliage starts to brown. At this time, you'll have to be tough and tear them out and replant with warm-season annuals, such as marigolds or petunias. But that's part of their charm—they are an ephemeral celebration of spring!

Planting Companions

Ornamental kale Kale and pansies can extend the bedding plant growing season for northern gardeners. They thrive in cool spring and fall temperatures and even withstand some frost.

Osteospermum Lavender osteospermum coordinates well with some lavender bicolor pansies.

Snapdragon Tall snapdragons make a striking backdrop for short pansies.

YOU — SHOULD KNOW — Viola flowers are edible and add color to salads and desserts. Don't use pesticides if you plan to eat them.

VARIETIES

1. 'BLUE & PURPLE RAIN' is an award-winning selection with purple flowers that age to white, then mature to purple and blue. It grows 12 inches tall and 16 inches wide.

2. 'BOWLES' BLACK' offers purple blooms that are so dark they appear black.

Plectranthus

Plectranthus selections

Light: **Partial Sun, Sun**
Height: **1–6 feet**
Width: **3–4 feet**
Color: **Green, Green/White, Green/Gold, Silver, Purple Foliage**
Bloom Time: **Fall; foliage looks good from spring through fall**
Special Features: **Fragrant, Good for Containers**

This vigorous foliage plant drapes neatly over container rims, making it ideal for window boxes, hanging baskets, and containers. Plectranthus is available with green or variegated foliage. Some varieties flower more than others. The foliage is also extremely fragrant. Plectranthus is a member of the mint family, but it doesn't have the same invasive character of mint. It can be easily controlled by cutting off new shoots. When the flower stalks have faded, simply cut them off to keep plants looking their best.

Planting Companions

Petunia Plectranthus provides unique foliage, and petunias provide the burst of color.

Coleus Plectranthus creates a miniature groundcover when planted at the feet of upright, bold-color coleus.

Osteospermum Lavender osteospermum looks lovely with purple-hue plectranthus such as 'Mona Lavender'.

VARIETIES

1. 'MONA LAVENDER' shows off rich purple leaves topped by spikes of lavender-purple flowers. It grows 28 inches tall and wide. It makes a lovely houseplant.

2. *PLECTRANTHUS ARGENTATUS* displays hairy, silvery leaves and is easy to grow indoors or out. It grows 3 feet tall and wide.

Wishbone Flower
Torenia fournieri selections

Light: **Shade, Partial Sun**
Height: **1–3 feet**
Width: **6–9 inches**
Color: **Yellow, Purple, White, Lavender**
Bloom Time: **Spring through Fall**
Special Features: **Deer Resistant, Good for Containers**

YOU
─ SHOULD KNOW ─
Keep wishbone flower in top shape by feeding every two weeks with a potassium-rich fertilizer.

Peek inside the two-lipped flowers and you'll see where the name comes from. Enchanting little wishbone flower, also dubbed clown flower, features vividly marked flowers that are said to resemble the face of a clown. It's a wonderful, relatively new choice for shade. The flower shape resembles tiny snapdragons, mouths wide open and showing off delicate throats marked with a contrasting color. Torenia grows easily from seed sown indoors in pots or outdoors in the ground. This little clown flower blooms nonstop until frost. From planting to frost, this showy flower brightens shady areas with a profusion of blooms. These undemanding heat- and humidity-tolerant plants maintain a glorious show without deadheading.

Planting Companions

Sweet alyssum Sweet alyssum in white or pastels combines well with the color spectrum offered by wishbone flower.

Begonia Fibrous-rooted begonia with white blooms and bronze foliage pairs beautifully planted with wishbone flower.

Impatiens Wishbone flower shines among a planting of impatiens in solid pink or white.

VARIETIES

1. 'CATALINA GILDED GRAPE' is a mounding selection featuring bright yellow flowers with purple throats. It grows 16 inches tall and trails 24 inches.

2. 'CATALINA WHITE LINEN' shows off lovely pure white flowers on a compact, mounding/trailing plant. It grows 16 inches tall and 24 inches across.

Bromeliad

Aechmea, Alcantarea, Ananas, Cryptanthus, Guzmania, Neoregelia, Tillandsia selections

Zones: **10–11**
Type: **Perennial**
Light: **Partial Shade**
Height: **Varies by Species**
Width: **Varies by Species**
Color: **Green, Red, Pink, Purple, Yellow**
Bloom Time: **Summer**
Special Features: **Good for Containers, Low Maintenance**

Blushing bromeliads are low-maintenance tropicals that make colorful, easy-care summer plants and houseplants. The plants have a rosette of serrated straplike leaves that form a cup in the center. Immature foliage is green, often striped with white or chartreuse, then when the plant is about to flower, the leaves develop a rosy hue, giving rise to the common name of blushing bromeliad. Small purple flowers develop in the cup, and they're secondary to the colorful leaves. Other bromeliads offer a variety of flower shapes and hues.

Planting Companions

Red pepper The fiery red peppers on hot pepper plants are a wonderful mixer with bromeliads.

Banana The giant leaves of banana, especially red-tip varieties, are dramatic with bromeliad, delivering a container with tropical punch.

Croton Beautiful tropical croton leaves come in a wide variety of splotchy colors that meld nicely with colorful bromeliads.

VARIETIES

1. 'RAPHAEL' BLUSHING BROMELIAD
Neoregelia 'Raphael' blushing bromeliad has deep green leaves with a narrow white margin.

2. 'STARLIGHT' _Aechmea_ 'Starlight' bears coral blooms and green, glossy spineless leaves.

Caladium
Caladium

Zones: **10–11**
Type: **Bulb**
Light: **Partial Shade, Shade, Sun**
Height: **8–20 inches**
Width: **24 inches**
Color: **Cream, Pink, Red, Silver, Green Foliage**
Bloom Time: **Foliage looks good from late spring through fall**
Special Features: **Good for Containers, Low Maintenance, Groundcover**

Providing color pizzazz in dim places where flowers can't, caladiums have come into their own recently with the popularity of tropical plants. The clumping, heart-shape leaves are available in a variety of veined patterns in many colors. Newer introductions bring caladiums out of the shade. The more substantial leaves of the Florida series, with greater heat tolerance, give the splashy caladiums their place in the sun. They look stunning in containers alone or combined with bright blooming annuals.

Planting Companions

Other caladiums Plant several bulbs with different colors of foliage in the same large container.

Elephant's ear Combine large, leafy elephant's ear and low-growing caladiums in a large container. The caladiums add a flounce of color to the exotic mix.

Begonia Shade-loving begonias in ruby red or clear pink are excellent mixers with complementary-color caladiums.

YOU
— SHOULD KNOW —
Tubers can be overwintered indoors then moved outdoors once temperatures stay above 60°F.

VARIETIES

1. 'FLORIDA CARDINAL' produces red heart-shape leaves broadly bordered in green. The plant grows 12 inches tall and is part of a thicker-leaved caladium series bred in Florida for sun tolerance. Zones 10–11

2. 'FLORIDA ELISE' bears vibrant splashes of silvery pink that highlight 16-inch-long leaves. This variety takes more sun than most and grows 2 feet tall. Zones 10–11

Croton

Codiaeum variegatum pictum

Zones: **10–11**
Type: **Perennial**
Light: **Light Shade, Sun**
Height: **1–8 feet**
Width: **1–3 feet**
Color: **Yellow, Green, Pink Foliage**
Bloom Time: **Foliage looks good all year**
Special Features: **Houseplant in Winter, Outdoor Container Plant in Summer**

Croton is a colorful shrublike plant with leathery leaves that are most vibrant in bright shade. They add instant structure and loads of color when placed in the center of a large container. In dense shade conditions, new leaves will be smaller and less intensely pigmented. Grow croton at 60°F to 85°F with high humidity.

Planting Companions

New Guinea impatiens Tall-growing crotons enjoy an underplanting of coordinating colorful New Guinea impatiens. Both species do well in shade.

Bromeliad Spiky, colorful bromeliads look smashing with painterly croton varieties.

Calibrachoa The small cascading flowers of calibrachoa are beautiful at the base of a croton plant; place in a sunny spot when pairing these two plants.

VARIETIES

1. 'ANDREW' is variegated with a wavy creamy yellow band around its leaf margin and a two-tone gray-green central leaf body.

2. 'RED ICETON' has foliage that emerges yellow or chartreuse and gradually turns gold with a wash of red.

Elephant's Ear
Alocasia

Zones: **7–11**
Type: **Bulb**
Light: **Shade, Partial Sun**
Height: **1–7 feet**
Width: **3–7 feet**
Color: **Green, White, Bronze, Maroon Foliage**
Bloom Time: **Foliage looks good from summer through fall**
Special Features: **Good for Containers, Low Maintenance**

Elephant's ears are big, dramatic, tropical-looking plants grown for their bold foliage. Aptly named, many bear triangular leaves that are leathery and uniquely textured. They grow well in large containers and can also be grown indoors as houseplants. The clumping foliage adds lush effects on porches and patios. Plants sprout from large bulbous roots and achieve maximum growth in warm, humid summer temperatures.

Planting Companions

Coleus For an all-foliage festival, combine color forms of coleus with the leafy charms of elephant's ear.

Caladium Large and colorful caladiums look stunning with equally impressive elephant's ear. Plant together in a large, colorful container and enjoy the textural interplay of the massive leaves.

Impatiens The bright pink or white flowers of impatiens contrast nicely with white-veined elephant's ear foliage.

YOU SHOULD KNOW Unpot and store these large bulbs at the end of the season. You can replant them next spring.

VARIETIES

1. AFRICAN MASK PLANT *Alocasia amazonica* is an exotic foliage plant featuring large leathery arrowhead leaves in shades of olive green, bronze, or maroon. It grows 3 feet tall. Zones 9–11

2. 'PURPLE PRINCE' *Alocasia grandis* 'Purple Prince' features 2- to 3-foot stems topped with gorgeous glossy white-veined leaves.

YOU
— SHOULD KNOW —
Pinch back Persian shield early in the growing season and for thicker, bushier foliage to follow.

Persian Shield
Strobilanthes dyerianus

Zones: **9–10**
Type: **Annual, Perennial**
Light: **Partial Shade, Sun**
Height: **2–3 feet**
Width: **2 feet**
Color: **Burgundy/Silver Foliage**
Bloom Time: **Foliage looks good spring through fall**
Special Features: **Good for Containers, Houseplant**

Persian shield's purple foliage shimmers with hints of green and silver on top, while the leaves' underside is solid maroon. The plant's large, showy almond-shape leaves deliver lots of pizzazz in a container. Use this lofty 2-to-3-foot-tall grower to add height to a pot. As the main plant in a container, it commands attention. Also nice is that its rich and dramatic color can be seen from far away. Plant with chartreuse-leaf or white-flowering companions to make the purple leaves really pop. Persian shield needs moisture and should be watered often; don't allow the soil to dry out. You can also enjoy this showy plant indoors. If keeping Persian shield as a houseplant, mist several times a week.

Planting Companions

Coleus Mix and match chartreuse and purple coleus with the leafy talents of Persian shield.

Lamb's-ears Soft, silvery leaves of lamb's-ears contrast well with the colorful leaves of Persian shield.

Impatiens Underplant pink-tinged Persian shield with a layer of pink impatiens for a perfect-in-pink combination.

Polka-Dot Plant

Hypoestes phyllostachya

Zones: **10–11**

Type: **Annual, Perennial**

Light: **Partial Shade**

Height: **10–12 inches**

Width: **9 inches**

Color: **White, Red, Pink, Green Foliage**

Bloom Time: **Foliage looks good spring through fall**

Special Features: **Good for Containers, Houseplant in Winter, Outdoor Container Plant in Summer**

The spotted foliage of polka-dot plant is marked with white, red, or pink dots; it's a gorgeous foliage plant for containers. This plant thrives in cramped quarters and humid conditions, preferring moist, rich soil. Water every other day, and give a monthly feeding. Polka-dot plant has a tendency to get leggy, especially in deep shade. To encourage tidy growth, pinch stem tips, remove flower spikes, and provide morning sun. Polka-dot plants are easily moved to indoor pots for winter.

Planting Companions

Hosta Large-leaf, single-color hostas combine well with the small, splashy leaves of polka-dot plant.

Coleus Create a color fantasy in a container with pink-hue coleus and polka-dot plant.

Impatiens Interplant pink impatiens with polka-dot plant for a beautiful pastel shade-loving combination.

YOU
__ SHOULD KNOW __
Before frost, remove polka-dot plants from containers and bring indoors. They make ideal houseplants.

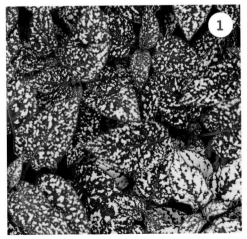

VARIETIES

1. WHITE POLKA-DOT PLANT Large pointed green leaves are splashed with bright white splotches. Plants grow 12 inches tall and 9 inches wide.

2. PINK POLKA-DOT PLANT Pretty green leaves are heavily blotched with pink. From afar, the leaves look almost all pink. This plant loves moist soil.

YOU SHOULD KNOW
Ajuga can be a vigorous spreader and can take light foot traffic.

Ajuga
Ajuga

Zones: **4–10**
Type: **Perennial**
Light: **Shade, Partial Shade, Sun**
Height: **Under 6 inches**
Width: **6–18 inches**
Color: **Blue, Pink, White Flowers; Purple/Burgundy, Green/Cream Foliage**
Bloom Time: **Spring, Summer**
Special Features: **Deer Resistant, Slope/Erosion Control, Low Maintenance, Good for Containers**

Ajuga is one of the most indispensable groundcovers around. It has many uses and stays in good shape much of the year. Also known as carpetweed or bugleweed, ajuga forms a 6-inch-tall mat of glossy leaves that always seem to look neat and fresh. In many cases, the leaves are colored with shades of purple, white, silver, cream, or pink. Individual plants grow as a rosette, and they intertwine to form a solid carpet that withstands some foot traffic. Blue, lavender, pink, or white flower spikes adorn plants spring to early summer. Ajuga is adaptable in rock gardens, in the front of beds and borders, under leggy shrubs or small trees, along paths, and just about any other place in the landscape you want to cover ground with attractive foliage and little flowers.

Planting Companions

Blue hosta Purple-leaf ajuga varieties complement blue-hue hostas.

Bleeding heart Early spring-blooming bleeding heart pairs with ajuga, which also rises and shines in early spring.

Coralbells The textural foliage of coralbells is a good combination plant with ajuga.

VARIETIES

1. 'BLACK SCALLOP' features shiny, dark purple leaves and springtime blue flowers. It's striking in containers. Zones 3–9

2. 'SILVER BEAUTY' is a quick-growing selection with silvery-green leaves edged in white. It bears small spikes of blue flowers in spring and grows 1 foot tall and 2 feet wide. Zones 3–9

Epimedium
Epimedium

Zones: **5–9**
Type: **Perennial**
Light: **Shade, Partial Shade**
Height: **Under 6 inches to 3 feet**
Width: **12–24 inches**
Color: **Red, Orange, Yellow, Pink, Purple, White Flowers; Chartreuse/Gold, Purple/Burgundy Foliage**
Bloom Time: **Spring**
Special Features: **Deer Resistant, Rabbit Resistant, Good for Containers, Drought Tolerant, Low Maintenance**

Epimedium, also called barrenwort or bishop's cap, is a shade plant that is underused in gardens. It is an asset to woodland gardens because it thrives in dry shade beneath shallow-rooted trees. It spreads at a moderate rate, forming a graceful, dense groundcover. Almost as a bonus, it produces dainty flowers shaped like a bishop's miter, prompting its common name bishop's cap. Its colorful foliage dangles on slender stalks, providing yet another less-common moniker: fairy wings. Some varieties are evergreen in mild-winter areas; others offer good fall color.

Planting Companions
Yellow corydalis Discover the delightful contrast of epimedium's shield-shape foliage against the lacy leaves of yellow corydalis.

Yellow variegated hosta Plant yellow-flowering epimedium with yellow variegated hostas for a beautiful yellow-on-yellow color vignette.

Ferns The lacy fronds of many kinds of ferns contrast nicely with the heart-shape leaves of epimedium.

YOU SHOULD KNOW
Divide epimedium plants after they flower in spring or wait until autumn.

VARIETIES

1. 'SULFUREUM' has whitish-yellow blooms with a yellow center and evergreen foliage. It reaches 8 to 12 inches tall. Zones 5–9

2. RED BARRENWORT *Epimedium rubrum* foliage is red along the edges and has rosy undertones. Color intensifies where it receives ample sun before trees leaf out in spring. Zones 4–9

Lamium (Spotted Deadnettle)
Lamium maculatum

Zones: **4–8**
Type: **Perennial**
Light: **Shade, Partial Shade**
Height: **6–12 inches**
Width: **6–12 inches**
Color: **Pink, White, Lavender Flowers; Silver-, White-, Yellow-Variegated Foliage**
Bloom Time: **Late May to Early Summer**
Special Features: **Deer Resistant, Drought Tolerant, Slope/Erosion Control, Good for Containers, Low Maintenance**

Free-blooming deadnettles enliven difficult places in sun or shade. From spring on, whorls of bright-color, two-lip flowers bloom abundantly on square stems. Triangular green leaves are splashed with silver or are silver-rimmed or veined with emerald. Deadnettles have unfairly gotten a bad name for being invasive and somewhat weedy, but they are easy to corral and should be cut back and deadheaded regularly. They're fine in partly shaded and shaded places where soil is well-drained yet retains moisture.

Planting Companions
Wild ginger In shade, evergreen European wild ginger forms low mats of glossy kidney-shape leaves that contrast well with the spotted deadnettle foliage.

Lilyturf In spring, the grasslike silver-and-white striped leaves of 'Silver Dragon' lilyturf add striking contrast to the leaves of spotted deadnettle.

Heart-leaf brunnera Blue-flowering brunnera produces clumps of heart-shape foliage that looks lovely with lamium.

VARIETIES

1. 'BEACON SILVER' *Lamium maculatum* 'Beacon Silver' has thick whorls of purple-pink two-lip flowers from spring through fall if deadheaded routinely and not allowed to desiccate. The small triangular leaves are mostly silver with a bright green edge. Zones 4–8

2. 'HERMANN'S PRIDE' *Lamium galeobdolon* 'Hermann's Pride' is more compact than the species. Its serrated leaves are crisply splashed with silver between the veins. In spring, whorls of yellow two-lip flowers bloom. Zones 4–8

Lilyturf
Liriope

Zones: **5–10**
Type: **Perennial**
Light: **Partial Shade, Shade, Sun**
Height: **Under 6 inches**
Width: **To 2 feet**
Color: **Blue, White Flowers; Green, Variegated Foliage**
Bloom Time: **Summer, Fall**
Special Features: **Deer Resistant, Drought Tolerant, Slope/ Erosion Control, Good for Containers, Low Maintenance**

Used often as a groundcover or an edging plant, liriope is popular for good reason. It stays green year-round in many climates, produces pretty blue or white flowers, and is about as tough a plant as you'll hope to meet. Its dense tufts of almost-evergreen, broadly grassy leaves are often striped. Stiff stems bear tight spikes of tiny blue or white bells, similar to those of grape hyacinth. It is best protected from drying winds in rich, well-drained soil that retains moisture. *Liriope muscari* grows in clumps that slowly expand. *Liriope spicata* can spread more aggressively.

Planting Companions

Japanese forestgrass Create a textural look by planting Japanese forestgrass with a deep green lilyturf.

Yellow coleus Accentuate the creamy variegation of striped liriope by planting it with yellow coleus.

Blue hosta Pair the grasslike foliage of green liriope with the green-blue, heart-shape leaves of hostas.

YOU SHOULD KNOW
Lilyturf can be a fast, almost aggressive spreader in ideal conditions.

VARIETIES

1. 'SILVER DRAGON' offers boldly variegated foliage and violet-blue blooms. Zones 6–11

2. LIRIOPE MUSCARI bears brilliant blue flower spikes among cream-edged strappy leaves in fall. Zones 5–10

Moneywort
Lysimachia nummularia

Zones: **3–10**
Type: **Perennial**
Light: **Shade, Partial Shade**
Height: **1–2 feet**
Width: **2 feet**
Color: **Light Green Foliage**
Bloom Time: **Foliage looks good from spring through fall**
Special Features: **Drought Tolerant, Good in Containers, Low Maintenance**

Moneywort, also called creeping Jenny, forms a dense green mat that cascades across the ground and over the edges of containers. It's especially nice in window boxes. This easy-care perennial produces a bounty of long, slender stems covered with dime-size leaves. Bright yellow cup-shape blooms emerge in summer to fall. Although plants may bloom, the foliage packs the biggest punch with this creeping beauty.

Planting Companions

Black mondograss The spiky black foliage of black mondograss contrasts nicely with the creeping habit and chartreuse foliage of moneywort.

Coleus Pair moneywort with purple and red varieties of coleus. The color combination is easy and eye-catching.

Hosta Variegated hosta varieties are lovely pot mates with moneywort.

VARIETIES

1. GOLDEN CREEPING JENNY *Lysimachia nummularia* 'Aurea' is a fast-growing groundcover for shade or partial shade. It bears round chartreuse foliage and grows 2 inches tall. It can spread indefinitely. Zones 4–8

2. CREEPING JENNY *Lysimachia nummularia* offers creeping green foliage that forms a dense mat. Fast-growing, it reaches just 2 inches but spreads quickly.

Toad Lily
Tricyrtis

Zones: **4–9**
Type: **Perennial**
Light: **Shade, Partial Shade**
Height: **1–3 feet**
Width: **1–2 feet**
Color: **Blue, White Flowers; Chartreuse/Gold Foliage**
Bloom Time: **Summer, Fall**
Special Features: **Deer Resistant, Drought Tolerant, Good in Containers, Low Maintenance, Cut Flowers**

No fall garden should be without toad lilies. These Asian curiosities bloom with orchidlike flowers that demand a close look when the garden is winding down in fall. They do best in light shade in humus-rich soil that retains moisture, and they're suitable for borders or less formal parts of the garden and among shrubs, gradually becoming large clumps. Some self-seed but not aggressively.

Planting Companions

Hosta Let toad lily rise up behind a clump of medium-size hostas. The leaves and flowers of toad lily are a beautiful contrast with hosta's large heart-shape leaves.

Fern-leaf bleeding heart The finely cut leaves of fern-leaf bleeding heart look beautiful paired with intricate flowers of toad lilies (they are beautiful together in a bouquet, too).

Liriope The strappy green foliage (which stays green year-round in many climates) pairs well with toad lily.

YOU SHOULD KNOW
The orchidlike flowers of toad lily make beautiful cut flowers.

VARIETIES

1. 'WHITE TOWERS' bears pure-white flowers in late summer and fall on 2-foot-tall stems. Zones 4–8

2. COMMON TOAD LILY (*Tricyrtis hirta*) has arching stems that bear clusters of upright flowers. The white orchidlike flowers are spotted with dark purple. It grows to 3-feet tall. Zones 4–9

YOU SHOULD KNOW

Prune vinca regularly to control it from wandering beyond the garden. Stems that reach the ground will root.

Vinca

Vinca minor

Zones: **4–11**
Type: **Perennial**
Light: **Shade, Partial Shade, Sun**
Height: **Under 6 inches to 3 feet**
Width: **Indefinitely Wide**
Color: **White, Lavender, Blue**
Bloom Time: **Spring, Summer, Fall**
Special Features: **Deer Resistant, Slope/Erosion Control, Good for Containers, Low Maintenance**

Vinca, also called periwinkle, is a fast-growing groundcover that is also prized as a trailer for containers and window boxes. In spring it produces 1-inch-wide funnel-shape flowers. The leaves of variegated types combine light and dark green, white, or yellow. Quick growth makes periwinkle an ideal coverage for any shaded or partially shaded location. Prepare the soil well prior to planting, and add humus to retain moisture. Keep the plants cut back to encourage bushy growth and keep them within bounds. Periwinkle can become invasive. Some vincas sold for pots are the species *Vinca major*, which is hardy only to Zone 7.

Planting Companions

Lungwort The silver-spotted hairy leaves of lungwort make an interesting contrast with dark evergreen periwinkle in shaded places.

Lilyturf Variegated lilyturf has upright clumps of strappy green leaves edged with cream, which show off well among the dark foliage of vinca in light shade.

Tiarella The white flowers of foamflower contrast nicely with the variegated leaves of vinca.

VARIETIES

1. PURPLE VINCA *Vinca minor* 'Atropurpurea' bears creeping stems and dark purple flowers on and off from spring to fall. Zones 4–9

2. VINCA MINOR *Vinca minor* offers pretty blue blooms periodically from spring to frost. Zones 4–9

Wild Ginger
Asarum canadense

Zones: **3–8**
Type: **Perennial**
Light: **Shade, Partial Shade**
Height: **Under 6 inches**
Width: **6–12 inches**
Color: **Green, Purple/Burgundy Foliage**
Bloom Time: **Spring**
Special Features: **Deer Resistant, Rabbit Resistant, Slope/Erosion Control, Low Maintenance, Good for Containers**

Wild ginger is a workhorse of a groundcover, spreading readily with beautifully glossy, slightly heart-shape leaves. It must have shade and moist, well-drained soil to thrive. With the right conditions, this native plant is indispensable, doing well where many other plants wouldn't. In spring it bears purplish maroon bell-shape blooms mostly hidden in the foliage. Hailing from the woodlands of North America, wild ginger produces fuzzy heart-shape leaves that keep a tidy appearance from spring to fall. This slow grower eventually forms an impressive clump.

Planting Companions

Fern-leaf bleeding heart Wild ginger looks beautiful with fern-leaf bleeding heart.

Astilbe Astilbe brings a graceful, feathering note to moist, shady landscapes. Ginger also prefers moist, shaded spots, so the two will grow happily together.

Japanese painted fern Washed with gorgeous silver and burgundy markings, Japanese painted ferns look beautiful with green wild ginger growing beneath.

YOU
— SHOULD KNOW —
Wild ginger's dark purple flowers are tucked neatly beneath the leaves, nearly out of sight.

VARIETIES

1. CANADIAN WILD GINGER (*Asarum canadense*) is a North American native with medium green downy leaves. It requires regular moisture to look its best. It has better heat tolerance than European wild ginger. Zones 2–8

2. EUROPEAN WILD GINGER (*Asarum europaeum*) bears striking evergreen leaves that have a glossy sheen. Zones 4–8

YOU
— **SHOULD KNOW** —
All azaleas are botanically classified as *Rhododendron*. The common name azalea refers to native deciduous species and some evergreen Asian types.

Azalea
Rhododendron

Zones: **3–9**
Light: **Partial Shade, Shade**
Height: **8–20 feet**
Width: **Up to 25 feet**
Color: **Blue, Green, Orange, Pink, Red, White Flowers; Chartreuse/Gold Foliage**
Bloom Time: **Spring, Fall**
Special Features: **Deer Resistant, Good for Privacy, Slope/Erosion Control, Fall Color**

Rhododendrons and azaleas belong to the genus *Rhododendron* and share many characteristics. Both groups thrive in well-drained acid soil and light shade. One point of difference is the shape of their flowers. Azaleas have funnel-shape blossoms, while rhododendrons have trumpet-shape flowers. Large leathery leaves that persist through winter also distinguish a rhododendron from the smaller azalea.

Although there are hundreds of species and varieties in the *Rhododendron* family, the most popular are noted for the brilliance and quantity of spring flower display.

From the giant rhododendrons of East Asian mountainsides to the rosebay rhododendron native to Eastern U.S. woodlands, this family of plants contains something for every landscape, if provided with moisture and shelter under trees. Many deciduous azaleas form flowers before the leaves unfurl.

Some azaleas bloom twice a season, on old wood in spring then on new wood in late summer to fall. To grow azaleas, ensure the plants receive adequate moisture and well-drained acidic soil.

VARIETIES

1. 'HERBERT' is an evergreen azalea with showy double flowers. It is a vigorous, well-branched plant that grows up to 5 feet tall and 6 feet wide. Zones 6–9

2. 'WHITE LIGHTS' produces creamy white flowers on tall upright bushes. Shrubs grow 5 feet tall and wide. Zones 4–9

Bottlebrush Buckeye

Aesculus parviflora

Zones: **4–8**
Light: **Partial Shade, Sun**
Height: **8–12 feet**
Width: **8–12 feet**
Color: **White**
Bloom Time: **Late Spring, Early Summer**
Special Features: **Fall Color, Low Maintenance, Slope/Erosion Control**

A native plant with bold presence, bottlebrush buckeye is a spreading, multistem shrub with large leaves and 8- to 12-inch-long bottlebrush-like flowers in early summer. It's an outstanding plant for mixed borders.

Choose a site with moist, well-drained soil that has plenty of organic matter. Growing 8 to 12 feet tall and wide, bottlebrush buckeye has an informal spreading habit that is especially striking when paired with upright needled evergreens and other plants with defined outlines.

Transplant container-grown or balled-and-burlapped plants in early spring. Water plants regularly for at least eight weeks after planting to ensure they develop a strong root system.

Bottlebrush buckeye rarely needs pruning because it is a slow-growing plant and naturally develops a graceful form. If necessary, prune in early spring. Rejuvenate plants by cutting stems back to ground level in early spring. This shrub has no significant pests.

There are no notable cultivars of bottlebrush buckeye readily available.

YOU
— SHOULD KNOW —
The bottlebrush's tall white flowers appear in late spring, which is much later than most other buckeyes.

YOU
SHOULD KNOW
Prevent winter leaf burn
(which turns leaves yellow)
by protecting boxwood plants
from drying winter winds.

Boxwood
Buxus species

Zones: **4–9**
Light: **Partial Shade, Sun**
Height: **1–10 feet**
Width: **1–5 feet**
Color: **White Flowers; Medium Green, Dark Green Foliage**
Bloom Time: **Spring**
Special Features: **Deer Resistant, Good for Containers, Slope/Erosion Control, Groundcover, Good for Privacy**

One of the most popular hedge plants, boxwood has lustrous evergreen leaves. With regular pruning, it can be sculpted into orbs, spires, cubes, and nearly any other shape you desire. A slow-growing plant, it has a pleasing shape when sheared just once a year.

Boxwood grows well in full sun or part shade and moist, well-drained soil. In warm climates, it thrives when provided a few hours of shade during the hottest part of the day. Drying winter winds are problematic in cold regions. Site plants near other shrubs or buildings where they will be protected from harsh winter winds.

Create a formal edge along a garden bed with a neat and tidy row of nearly round boxwood. Or add easy-care structure to a mixed border with a pyramidal boxwood. Choose a cultivar that has a mature size appropriate for the intended planting location.

Transplant container-grown plants in spring. Water plants regularly for at least eight weeks after transplanting to promote a strong root system. Keep boxwood's root zone cool by spreading a 2-inch layer of organic mulch, such as cocoa hulls or shredded bark, over the area. Prune boxwood anytime from spring to midsummer. Do not prune plants in fall because pruning will spur tender new growth that can be damaged by cold winter temperatures. Gas-powered or electric shears make efficient work of pruning a boxwood hedge.

VARIETIES

1. 'CHICAGOLAND GREEN' is prized for keeping its green color through winter. It grows 2 to 3 feet tall and wide.

2. 'GREEN MOUNTAIN' grows in a pyramidal shape, 5 feet tall and 3 feet wide.

3. 'GREEN MOUND' is a hardy cultivar that grows 3 feet tall and wide.

4. 'GOLDEN TRIUMPH' is a low-growing mounded plant with showy golden yellow leaf margins. It grows 3 feet tall and wide.

Camellia
Camellia species

Zones: **6–9**
Light: **Shade, Partial Shade**
Height: **5–20 feet**
Width: **To 20 feet**
Color: **Orange, Pink, Red, White**
Bloom Time: **Fall, Winter, Spring**
Special Features: **Good for Privacy, Good for Containers, Cut Flowers, Low Maintenance**

Referred to as the rose of winter, camellia adds striking beauty to the sleepy winter landscape. Cup-shape, multipetal flowers adorn small to medium evergreen shrubs for weeks. When not in bloom, camellia's glossy green foliage is a good backdrop for other plants.

Camellias grow best in moist, well-drained soil that is rich in organic matter. They languish in dry, sandy soil and should not be planted in such sites. Camellias prefer partial shade; a site with morning sun and dense afternoon shade is best. These slow-growing shrubs fare particularly well in the shade of pines. In Zone 7, site camellias in microclimates where they will be protected from extreme winter conditions. Protected areas along evergreen hedges, brick walls, and the side of a building will limit winter damage.

Very slow growing, they put on a few inches of new growth a year and are easy to maintain at a small stature. Camellia flower colors range from white to red and include variegated blossoms.

Transplant container-grown plants in spring. Water for at least eight weeks after transplanting to encourage plants to develop a strong root system. Spread a 2-inch-deep layer of organic mulch, such as pine straw, over the shrub's root zone to limit moisture loss and keep roots cool in the heat of summer.

If necessary, prune camellias after bloom. Because they are slow growing, they rarely need pruning. Leaf spot diseases and numerous scale insects attack camellias. The best defense against these pests is to promote healthy, vigorous growth. Water plants during extended dry periods, and renew the mulch layer annually.

YOU SHOULD KNOW
There are more than 2,000 camellia cultivars. Many perform best in a specific region. Talk to local garden centers to find varieties that do best in your region.

VARIETIES

1. 'APPLE BLOSSOM' has pearly white blooms that are edged with pink. It blooms in midwinter. Its dense habit makes it a good choice for a hedge. It grows 10 feet tall and wide.

2. 'PEARL MAXWELL' has double shell-pink blooms in late winter and glossy green foliage. It grows 6 to 8 feet tall and wide.

3. 'PINK PERFECTION' has cotton candy-pink blossoms and dark green foliage. It blooms in mid- to late winter. It grows 6 to 8 feet tall and wide.

4. 'YULETIDE' has showy red blooms with bold yellow centers. It flowers in midwinter. It grows 8 to 10 feet tall and wide.

YOU
— SHOULD KNOW —
Daphnes generally don't tolerate transplanting, so don't move the shrub once it is established.

SHRUBS

Daphne
Daphne species

Zones: **4–9**
Light: **Light Shade, Sun**
Height: **2–4 feet**
Width: **2–4 feet**
Color: **Pink, White Flowers; Green, Variegated Foliage**
Bloom Time: **Spring, Fall**
Special Features: **Fragrant, Compact, Good for Containers**

Welcome winter or spring with daphne's sweetly fragrant flowers. Particular about its growing conditions, daphne demands moist, well-drained soil and partial shade. Grow it near an entryway or outdoor living area to enjoy its scent.

A structural plant for partial shade, daphne thrives in moist, well-drained soil that is rich in organic matter. Daphne is notorious for being a short-lived shrub.

Semievergreen, evergreen, and deciduous, daphnes are mounded plants that usually grow 2 to 4 feet tall and wide. Some species have small leaves that add fine, airy texture to the landscape.

Transplant container-grown plants in spring. Spread a 2-inch layer of mulch over the root zone to keep soil cool and moist. Water plants regularly after planting, and continue watering as needed during dry conditions.

Prune daphne in early summer. Plants respond well to annual pruning. Several pests attack daphne, but none are serious.

VARIETIES

1. **'CAROL MACKIE'** has pink flowers and variegated leaves. It is semievergreen and a reliable plant for foundation plantings. Zones 5–8

2. **'SUMMER ICE'** bears long-blooming white flowers with a flush of pink. Flowers are borne in clusters at the end of the branch. Zones 6–8

Fothergilla
Fothergilla species

Zones: **5–8**
Light: **Partial Shade, Sun**
Height: **2–8 feet**
Width: **2–8 feet**
Color: **White Flowers; Red, Orange Foliage**
Bloom Time: **Spring**
Special Features: **Fall Foliage, Good for Containers, Fragrant**

One of the best native shrubs for fall color, fothergilla has a tidy round shape and sweetly fragrant flowers in spring. This multiseason plant is perfect for foundation plantings and mixed borders, and it's also a good addition to containers.

Fothergilla grows best in full sun or partial shade. It flowers more prolifically and develops better fall color in full sun. For best results, it requires moist, well-drained soil that has plenty of organic matter.

A small to medium shrub, fothergilla grows 2 to 8 feet tall and wide. Its leathery dark green leaves turn hot shades of yellow, orange, and scarlet in fall. Before leaves emerge in spring, the plant debuts bottlebrush-like white flowers. The fragrant flowers perfume the garden.

Transplant container-grown plants in spring. Water plants regularly for at least eight weeks after transplanting to ensure they develop a strong root system. Fothergilla rarely requires pruning. If necessary, prune in late spring after blooms fade. Plants are generally pest-free.

YOU
_ SHOULD KNOW _
Fothergilla has beautiful fall color, but plants grown in the shade will be less vivid

VARIETIES

1. 'MT. AIRY' has blue-green summer foliage and consistent yellow-orange and red fall color. Zones 4–9

2. LARE FOTHERGILLA *Fothergilla major* is an ideal background shrub for the shade garden that grows 8 feet tall and wide. Native to areas of North America. Zones 5–9

YOU
— **SHOULD KNOW** —
Like most rhododendrons and azaleas, mountain laurel needs soil with an acidic pH.

Mountain Laurel

Kalmia latifolia

Zones: **5–9**
Light: **Partial Shade, Sun**
Height: **8–20 feet**
Width: **To 12 feet**
Color: **Pink, Red, White**
Bloom Time: **Spring**
Special Features: **Deer Resistant, Good for Containers**

A North American native, mountain laurel has magnificent flowers and leathery evergreen foliage. It's a colorful plant for partial shade and mixed shrub borders. Or use it at the back of a perennial border.

Plant mountain laurel in full sun or part shade and moist, acidic, well-drained soil.

Mountain laurel is a slow-growing plant and will take many years to reach its mature size. Several dwarf cultivars are available, making it possible to grow this shrub with multiseason interest in small-space gardens or large containers.

Transplant container-grown plants in spring. Mountain laurel thrives in cool, moist soil. Spread a 2-inch-thick layer of organic mulch over the plant's root zone to keep roots cool and prevent soil moisture loss.

Prune plants in summer after flowers fade. Leaf spot, blight, and a few other pests attack mountain laurel, but vigorous plants usually fend them off without excessive damage.

VARIETIES

1. 'OLYMPIC FIRE' This gorgeous shrub shows off red-pink buds that open to dark pink flowers. It grows 10 feet tall and wide. Zones 5–9

2. 'ELF' The first dwarf mountain laurel introduced, 'Elf' has large pink buds that open to nearly white flowers. It grows 3 feet tall and 4 feet wide. Zones 5–9

Hydrangea
Hydrangea species

Zones: **3–9**

Light: **Partial Shade, Shade, Sun**

Height: **3–20 feet**

Width: **3–18 feet**

Color: **White, Blue, Pink, Red, Yellow, Light Green Flowers; Chartreuse, Green Foliage**

Bloom Time: **Summer, Fall**

Special Features: **Fall Foliage, Cut Flowers, Good for Containers,**

Hydrangeas, which come in types that can flourish in sun or shade, offer huge bouquets of clustered flowers from summer through fall. Varieties of hydrangea differ in size of plant and flower shape, flower color, and bloom time.

Macrophyllas feature two main groups: mopheads and lacecaps. Mophead hydrangeas offer big dome-shape clusters of flowers in blue, pink, or white. Most mopheads bloom in late spring or early summer but make flower buds the year before you see them. Prune them in early summer, right after the flowers fade. Lacecap hydrangeas give the garden a delicate look, forming a flower head composed of a ring of colorful florets surrounding a lacy cluster of small florets. Lacecap hydrangeas have similar cultural needs as their mophead cousins, mainly differing in flower form.

PeeGee hydrangeas grow into small trees; the flowers turn russet and cling into winter. Oakleaf hydrangeas have the most handsome foliage, which reddens dramatically in fall. Some newer hydrangeas feature huge flowers on compact plants, ideal for containers and small gardens.

Choosing the right hydrangea for your landscape begins with choosing a plant hardy in your area. Gardeners in cold-winter areas can grow smooth, panicle, oakleaf, and a few bigleaf hydrangeas. Gardeners in warm-winter areas have most success with bigleaf and oakleaf hydrangeas. Panicle hydrangeas are the most adaptable and best suited for harsh climates or growing conditions.

**YOU
— SHOULD KNOW —**
Mophead and many lacecap hydrangeas are sensitive to soil pH. In acidic soils, flowers tend to blue; in more alkaline soils, blooms tend toward pink.

VARIETIES

1. ENDLESS SUMMER is an easy-to-grow bigleaf hydrangea (*Hydrangea macrophylla*) for cold regions. It blooms on new and old wood, ensuring flowers even when the winters are particularly cold. It grows 3 to 5 feet tall and wide. Zones 4–9

2. 'TWIST-N-SHOUT' is a lacecap type of *Hydrangea macrophylla* that bears pink-and-purple flowers on new wood. It grows 3 to 5 feet tall and wide. Zones 4–9

3. 'LIMELIGHT' is a *Hydrangea paniculata* type that is sun-loving with large green flowers that appear midsummer into autumn. The blooms deepen to pink in cool weather. It grows 8 feet tall and 6 feet wide. Zones 3-8

4. 'LEMON DADDY' is a bold-color shrub for brightening a dark corner. Grown more for its chartreuse foliage than its flowers, it has bright green leaves from early spring through fall. 3 to 5 feet tall and wide. Zones 6–9

YOU
_ SHOULD KNOW _
Rhododendrons and azaleas are both classified as *Rhododendron,* however the name rhododendron refers to species that have large, leathery evergreen leaves.

Rhododendron
Rhododendron species

Zones: **4–9**
Light: **Partial Shade, Shade**
Height: **2–20 feet**
Width: **10–15 feet**
Color: **White, Pink, Red, Orange**
Bloom Time: **Mid- to Late Spring, Fall**
Special Features: **Deer Resistant, Good for Privacy, Slope/Erosion Control, Fragrance**

Rhododendrons are some of the most popular flowering shrubs. Their colorful flower clusters decorate the evergreen or deciduous plants for weeks in spring. Lovely plants for partial shade, rhododendrons add color to sun-dappled beds and borders.

There are many species and varieties of rhododendron, including some that are native to North America. They thrive in moist, well-drained, acidic soil that is rich in organic matter. Planting sites near pine trees are particularly suitable because the soil tends to be acidic.

Most plants do well when planted where they will receive morning sun and afternoon shade. Plant rhododendrons on the north or east side of a house for a pleasing mix of sun and shade.

Rhododendrons range from small plants that are 2 feet tall and wide to large shrubs growing 15 to 20 feet tall and 10 to 15 feet wide. They have a round and irregular outline. Rhododendrons bloom in mid- to late spring. Some new varieties bloom again in early fall.

Plant container-grown rhododendrons in spring. The plants have fibrous root systems that are easy to transplant. The threadlike roots also dry out quickly; be sure to water plants regularly for at least eight weeks after transplanting. Blanket the soil over the root zone with a 2-inch layer of organic mulch. Pine straw is best because it will provide valuable nutrients as it breaks down and contributes to the acidic nature of the soil around plants. Some growers suggest fertilizing plants with a product designed especially for rhododendrons, but it is not necessary for a healthy plant.

Rhododendrons and azaleas are slow growing and rarely require extensive pruning. Prune plants after the blooms fade in late spring. Several insects and diseases affect rhododendrons and azaleas. Lacebugs are particularly troublesome. Healthy, vigorous plants usually shrug off pests.

VARIETIES

1. 'CAPISTRANO' is a compact, mounding selection to 4 feet tall and wide, bearing trusses of frilled greenish-yellow flowers. Zones 6–8

2. 'BOULE DE NEIGE' translates from French to "ball of snow" which is what the blooms look like in spring. This rhododendron has a compact growth habit and loves deep shade. Zones 4–8

3. 'OLGA MEZITT' is an evergreen selection that produces small trusses of deep peach-pink flowers. The leaves redden in fall. It grows to 4 feet tall and wide. Zones 4–8

4. 'NOVA ZEMBLA' is a large evergreen shrub that bears trusses of deep red flowers with spotted throats. It grows 5 to 10 feet tall and wide. Zones 5–8

5. 'ENGLISH ROSEUM' has large clusters of lavender-pink flowers. 5 to 10 feet tall and wide. Zones 4–8

6. KURUME HYBRIDS is a popular group of evergreen rhododendrons. Plants include a rainbow of flower colors. 3 to 5 feet tall and wide. Zones 6–9

7. 'SUN CHARIOT' is an upright, dense-growing spring-blooming variety that grows 6 feet tall and wide. It bears yellow blooms with orange blotches in large clusters. Zones 6–9

8. 'HAAGA' has massive clusters of pink flowers. It grows best in cool regions. 3 feet tall and wide. Zones 4–8

Viburnum
Viburnum species

Zones: **2–9**
Light: **Partial Shade, Sun**
Height: **3–20 feet**
Width: **5–12 feet**
Color: **White, Pink Flowers; Red Berries**
Bloom Time: **Spring**
Special Features: **Fall Color, Deer Resistant, Drought Tolerant, Good for Privacy, Slope/Erosion Control, Attracts Birds, Low Maintenance**

North American natives with outstanding flowers, intense fragrance, and fruit that delights wildlife, viburnums are an essential part of many landscapes. Use them as focal points in mixed borders, or plant them en masse to create an informal hedge that will beckon birds.

Viburnums thrive in moist, well-drained soil and full sun or partial shade. They are an adaptable group of shrubs, growing in a variety of landscape situations. Once established, they tolerate drought well. They also grow well in heavy soil provided standing water is not present.

Some viburnums are far too large for today's landscapes. Many new small cultivars make it possible to enjoy a greater number of these easy-to-grow plants. Some sport fragrant flowers; others have flowers with virtually no scent. White is the most common flower color, although some species have pink-tinged blooms. Most viburnums produce fruit that attracts wildlife, and fall leaf color is often notable.

Transplant container-grown or balled-and-burlapped plants in spring or early summer. Water plants regularly for at least six weeks after transplanting to encourage them to develop a strong root system.

Prune viburnums as needed to maintain desired size. Plants generally develop a pleasing shape without pruning. If pruning is necessary, do so in late spring or early summer after flowers fade. For a natural appearance, selectively remove one-third of the oldest stems and trim back remaining stems as needed.

Viburnums are generally pest-free. Adequate moisture promotes strong, healthy growth that thwarts most pest attacks. Water viburnums deeply if a drought extends for more than two weeks during the growing season.

YOU
_ SHOULD KNOW _
Viburnums offer four-season appeal: flowers in spring, berries in summer, fall color, and interesting bark in winter.

VARIETIES

1. 'MOHAWK' (*V. × burkwoodii*) has spicy-scented white flowers in mid-spring that are followed by red fruit that changes to black at maturity. It has brilliant red flower buds and striking orange-red fall color. 8 to 10 feet tall and 5 to 7 feet wide. Zones 5–8

2. AMERICAN CRANBERRYBUSH (*V. trilobum*) has shiny dark green leaves that turn yellow or red-purple in fall. Its large white flat-top flowers are followed by bright red fruit that remains on the plant through much of the winter. 8 to 12 feet tall and wide. 'Compactum' is a good choice for small landscapes—it grows 6 feet tall and wide. Zones 2–7

3. DOUBLEFILE VIBURNUM (*V. plicatum tomentosum*) has red-purple fall color and showy white flowers. 8 to 10 feet tall and wide. 'Shasta' has abundant 6-inch-wide white flower clusters. Zones 5–7

4. 'BLUE MUFFIN' (*V. dentatum*) has large white flower clusters and copious quantities of blue berries in fall. The fruit is relished by wildlife. As an arrowwood viburnum, it is one of the most adaptable viburnums, growing in urban and difficult conditions. 6 to 8 feet tall and wide. Zones 3–8

5. 'CAYUGA' (*V. carlesii*) has good disease resistance and large flowers. A Koreanspice viburnum, it is known for its fragrant pinkish-white flower clusters. 4 to 6 feet tall and wide. Zones 5–7

6. LEATHERLEAF VIBURNUM (*V. rhytidophyllum*) will retain most of its dark green leaves in cold climates and is evergreen in the South. It has large flat-top yellow-white flowers. It is a useful shrub for hedges and screens. 10 to 15 feet tall and wide. Zones 5–9

YOU
— SHOULD KNOW —
Witch hazel flowers are fragrant. Cut branches in early spring for gorgeous bouquets.

Witch hazel

Hamamelis

Zones: **3–9**
Light: **Partial Shade, Sun**
Height: **8–20 feet**
Width: **10–20 feet**
Color: **Yellow, Red, Orange Flowers; Chartreuse/Gold Foliage**
Bloom Time: **Late Winter**
Special Features: **Fall Color, Low Maintenance, Good for Privacy, Fragrant**

Blooming in late winter, witch hazel's color-rich red or yellow flowers add beauty and fragrance at a time when the landscape is still cloaked in drab winter tones. Many cultivars have good fall color. Use witch hazel in a mixed shrub border.

Witch hazel grows best in moist, well-drained soil that is rich in organic matter. It thrives in full sun or partial shade.

A large shrub with an open, irregular outline, witch hazel often grows 10 to 20 feet tall and wide. The branches have a wide, spreading habit, giving the plant an informal appearance. Witch hazel blooms for several weeks between January and mid-March. Its medium-green leaves reliably turn warm shades of yellow, red, and orange in fall.

Transplant container-grown plants in spring. Prune witch hazel as needed in late spring after flowers fade. Plants are rarely troubled by pests.

VARIETIES

1. 'ARNOLD'S PROMISE' boasts a copious display of clear yellow flowers in spring. It rivals forsythia in flower power and is very fragrant. Zones 5–9

2. 'SANDRA' *Hamamelis vernalis* 'Sandra' offers golden-yellow flowers in late winter or early spring and yellow autumn foliage. It grows 10 feet tall and wide. Zones 4–8

Yew

Taxus species

Zones: **2–7**
Light: **Shade, Partial Shade, Sun**
Height: **2–20 feet**
Width: **2–20 feet**
Color: **Green Foliage; Red Berries**
Bloom Time: **Not Applicable**
Special Features: **Deer Resistant, Drought Tolerant, Good for Privacy, Slope/Erosion Control, Groundcover, Low Maintenance**

Among the best evergreen shrubs for landscapes, yews are slow-growing and disease-resistant. They have excellent dark green color and are available in many shapes and sizes. For a fresh, modern look, pair them with perennials.

Yews grow equally well in sun or shade. These shrubs demand soil with excellent drainage. Anything less than well-drained soil will result in root rot and plant death. A loose, rich soil is best.

There is wide variation in plant size and shape. Nearly all cultivars are compact and retain dense character with age without extensive pruning. Yews can be maintained at 2 feet tall and wide or allowed to surpass 20 feet tall and wide, depending on cultivar.

Transplant container-grown or balled-and-burlapped plants in spring. Prune as needed in early spring to maintain the desired size and shape. Deer browse yews.

Yews are among the most toxic plants, yet they are rarely problematic in a residential landscape. The foliage, bark, and seeds are all poisonous. Yew's red berries contain seeds, which are toxic, but the fleshy red seed covering is not toxic. The seeds are not digested by the human body and pass through harmlessly.

YOU SHOULD KNOW
Yews come in a wide variety of shapes and sizes, and they can easily be sheared into hedges or screens.

VARIETIES

1. HICKS YEW (*Taxus media* 'Hicksii') is a fast-growing hybrid with an open habit ideal for hedges. It's also a hardier substitute for Irish yew. This variety grows 25 feet tall by 10 feet wide. Zones 5–7

2. 'CAPITATA' (*Taxus cuspidata* 'Capitata') forms a broad, dense pyramid, slow growing to 40 feet tall. Zones 4–7

YOU
— SHOULD KNOW —
Buckeyes produce attractive shiny brown nuts that are inedible.

Buckeye
Aesculus species

Zones: **4–8**
Light: **Partial Shade, Sun**
Height: **8–70 feet**
Width: **12–15 feet**
Color: **Red, Pink, Yellow, White Flowers**
Bloom Time: **Spring**
Special Features: **Attracts Birds, Low Maintenance**

Buckeyes have a bold presence in the landscape. They add color with tropical-looking spring flowers and pumpkin-orange to yellow or brown fall foliage. Use large buckeyes, also called horse chestnuts, as shade trees in medium to large yards.

Buckeyes grow best in full sun or part shade and tolerate shade better than many other tree species. Moist, well-drained, deep, fertile soil is best for buckeyes. Most do not adapt well to difficult growing conditions and are likely to balk at slow-draining clay soil or urban situations.

Most buckeyes develop into large, stately trees. Be sure to plant them where they will have plenty of space to grow. There is great variety within the buckeye group. Some selections top out at 15 to 20 feet tall, while others rise to more than 70 feet. Most trees have a rounded, spreading habit with a hint of horizontal branching.

Buckeyes bloom in late spring in shades of white, yellow-green, or red. The 6- to 8-inch-long flower clusters appear after the leaves have expanded. Smooth round fruit, often called buckeyes, ripen inside hard seed coats in fall. In autumn, buckeye foliage varies from dull brown to shades of yellow and pumpkin orange. Fall color is variable from year to year.

Plant container-grown or balled-and-burlapped plants in early spring. Spread a 2-inch layer of organic mulch under the tree canopy to aid in soil moisture retention. Water regularly for two to three months after transplanting.

Prune buckeye in late winter or early spring. Various leaf diseases affect these trees. Leaf blotch is common in summer. It appears as small brown spots on the leaves. The spots expand to create large blotches, and eventually the leaves fall. Drought contributes to leaf blotch as well as makes trees susceptible to other pests such as Japanese beetle, bagworms, and canker. Water buckeyes deeply and infrequently during extended periods of drought.

VARIETIES

1. OHIO BUCKEYE (*A. glabra*) does not have prominent flowers. It is troubled by leaf diseases. 20 to 40 feet tall and wide. Zones 3–7

2. RED BUCKEYE (*A. pavia*) thrives in light shade. It has dark green leaves, rich red flowers, and a round habit. Moist soil is essential. 15 to 20 feet tall and wide. Zones 4–8

3. RED HORSE CHESTNUT (*A. × carnea*) has a rounded outline and a dense canopy. Rose-red flowers cover the tree in late spring. It is adaptable to a wide range of soils. 30 to 40 feet tall and wide. Zones 4–7

4. YELLOW BUCKEYE (*A. flava*) is a native horse chestnut that is notably trouble-free. It has yellow flowers and is adaptable to most conditions. 60 to 75 feet tall and 30 to 50 feet wide. Zones 4–8

Dogwood
Cornus species

Zones: **3–8**
Light: **Partial Shade, Sun**
Height: **8–20 feet**
Width: **To 20 feet**
Color: **White**
Bloom Time: **Spring**
Special Features: **Good for Privacy, Attracts Birds, Good for Containers, Slope/Erosion Control**

Prized for profuse blooms and horizontal branching pattern, dogwood trees are a pleasing complement to strong vertical elements such as buildings, fences, and upright trees. Valuable multiseason plants, they are excellent trees for residential landscapes.

Ever-popular flowering dogwood (*C. florida*) is an understory tree preferring to grow in dappled shade. It thrives in moist, rich, well-drained soil and is a good choice for the north or east side of a structure. It will also grow well in the shade of existing trees, provided the soil is moist and well-drained. Zones 5–9.

Kousa dogwood (*C. kousa*) is more tolerant of intense light and grows well in full sun or part shade. Moist, rich, well-drained soil is ideal. Zones 5–8. Pagoda dogwood (*C. alternifolia*) grows as a large multistemmed shrub or a small tree. It grows best in moist, acidic, well-drained soils and partial shade. Its horizontal branches give it a layered appearance. Its showy white flowers are held above foliage for several days in May or June.

Flowering and kousa dogwoods grow 20 feet tall and wide. Usually multistem trees, they often have low branches and grow slowly. Many other forms of dogwood have shrublike habits. Dogwoods bloom in mid-spring, and their glistening red fruit ripens in September. Birds often devour the juicy fruit. Medium green summer foliage turns shades of yellow, red, and orange in autumn.

Plant container-grown or balled-and-burlapped dogwoods in spring. Plant flowering dogwood in partial shade; plants growing in full sun quickly fail. Spread a 2- to 3-inch-deep layer of compost or organic mulch over the soil under the canopy to prevent moisture loss.

Prune dogwoods lightly, if needed, in late spring after flowers fade. Pruning is rarely required. Several pests, including powdery mildew and borers, infect dogwoods. Thwart pests by promoting plant health.

YOU SHOULD KNOW
One of the most beautiful spring bloomers, dogwood has brilliant flowers that are highly visible even when growing beneath other trees.

VARIETIES

1. 'CLOUD 9' is a prolific bloomer that begins flowering at a young age. 15 feet tall and wide. Zones 5–9

2. CHEROKEE BRAVE has unique pink flowers and bronze-red new foliage that turns green. 20 feet tall and wide. Zones 5–9

3. 'WOLF EYES' has variegated leaves and pink to red fall color. It tends to be more shrub than tree. 6 feet tall and wide. Zones 5–8

4. 'SATOMI' is a slow-growing cultivar with pink flowers. 20 feet tall and 15 feet wide. Zones 5–8

YOU
_ SHOULD KNOW _
Plant false cypress in containers to add a formal look to patios and porches.

False Cypress
Chamaecyparis

Zones: **5–9**
Light: **Partial Shade, Sun**
Height: **8–20 feet**
Width: **15–30 feet**
Color: **Green, Light Green, Silver, Blue Foliage**
Bloom Time: **Foliage looks good year-round**
Special Features: **Good for Privacy, Groundcover, Good for Containers, Attracts Birds**

Incomparable texture and color intensity make false cypress a valuable companion in landscapes and containers. They come in a wide range of sizes, which makes them very adaptable for large or small landscapes.

Group false cypress to create an attractive hedge or screen. The fanlike boughs hold long, soft needles that resemble filigreed lace or ferns. The upswept branches of Hinoki cypress look like a Japanese painting, while the Nootka false cypress features pendulous branches.

The color range of false cypress extends from blue-gray to deep green to gold. A moist, slightly acidic soil is ideal for these trees; they do not thrive in hot and dry or windy conditions.

Sawara false cypress is sometimes called threadleaf false cypress for its delicate-looking foliage; this slow-growing evergreen usually matures at 20 feet tall. Many cultivars with slight variations in foliage color and plant form are available.

VARIETIES

1. 'BABY BLUE' *Chamaecyparis pisifera* 'Baby Blue' is a compact selection that forms a dense shrub of silvery-blue foliage. It grows 6 feet tall and 4 feet wide. Zones 4–8

2. 'CRIPSII' *Chamaecyparis obtusa* 'Cripsii' features golden foliage that deepens to dark green. Zones 4–8

Hornbeam
Carpinus species

Zones: **3–9**
Light: **Partial Shade, Sun**
Height: **To 20 feet**
Width: **To 50 feet**
Color: **Chartreuse/Gold Foliage**
Bloom Time: **Not Applicable**
Special Features: **Good for Privacy, Fall Color**

A diverse group of small to medium trees, hornbeams have clean green foliage and refined elegance. Use these easy-to-grow plants as screens, as hedges, or in groups to soften the side of a building. In fall, foliage reliably turns a pleasing shade of yellow-brown.

Hornbeams grow best in full sun but tolerate light to moderate shade. Plants thrive in well-drained soil.

European hornbeam (*C. betulus*) is an excellent choice for residential landscapes. It grows 30 to 40 feet tall and wide. American hornbeam (*C. caroliniana*) grows 20 to 30 feet tall and wide and is well-suited to naturalized planting areas. An adaptable tree sadly overlooked by gardeners, American hornbeam is a slow-growing small tree with strong wood. In fall, the foliage turns shades of yellow, orange, and red; in winter, the fluted texture of the bark gives hornbeam one of its other common names: musclewood.

Hornbeams tolerate pruning so well that small trees can be sculpted into long-lasting hedges. Prune plants in late winter or early spring. Hornbeams have no notable pests.

YOU SHOULD KNOW
Native to areas of North America, hornbeam can be grown with a single trunk or a clump of smaller trunks.

VARIETIES

1. EUROPEAN HORNBEAM (*Carpinus betulus*) 'Columnaris' has closely spaced upright growth, making it a good hedge or screen plant.

2. AMERICAN HORNBEAM offers beautiful red-orange fall color.

YOU
─ SHOULD KNOW ─
Japanese maples don't like wind; plan to position them in a protected location.

Japanese Maple
Acer

Zones: **3–9**
Light: **Partial Shade, Sun**
Height: **3–15 feet**
Width: **10–12 feet**
Color: **Red, Green, Chartreuse, Burgundy, Variegated Foliage**
Bloom Time: **Foliage looks good from spring through fall**
Special Features: **Good for Containers, Attracts Birds, Fall Color**

Japanese maples have it all! They feature an exquisitely layered cascading form, an elegant fine leaf texture, and remarkable fall color. Among the many varieties, there are maples with yellow-green, purple, red, bronze, and variegated leaves. And sizes suit any landscape, varying from 3-foot dwarfs to slow-growing 15-footers.

Many Japanese maples have a wonderful way of spreading in the shape of low graceful domes. On a slope or overhang, arching branches can descend even below the base of the trunk.

Japanese maples can get a little pricey, so consider them an investment in your landscape. Elegant Japanese maples also make excellent container plants. The sweet spot for Japanese maples is Zones 6–8. But you can still enjoy these coveted trees in both hotter and colder climates.

Japanese maples are fairly heat tolerant. References often list them as hardy up to Zone 7 or 8, but many gardeners successfully grow them in higher Zones. However, in hot, dry climates, leaves will often scorch, therefore protection from the afternoon sun is important. Under a pergola or on the east or north side of a house is ideal. Also, green-leaf varieties—less popular but just as garden-worthy as purple types—may be a little less susceptible to leaf scorch than purple-leaf varieties. Either way, maples in arid climates require regular summer irrigation.

VARIETIES

1. 'BENI SCHICHIHENGE' *Acer palmatum*
'Beni Schichihenge' bears green leaves edged in pink and cream. They turn shades of yellow in fall. This tree grows 8 feet tall and wide. Zones 6–9

2. 'DISSECTUM ATROPURPUREUM' *Acer palmatum* 'Dissectum Atropurpureum' bears broad arching branches with finely textured reddish-purple leaves. It grows 8 feet tall and 10 feet wide. Zones 6–8

Redbud
Cercis canadensis

Zones: **4–9**
Light: **Partial Shade, Sun**
Height: **8–30 feet**
Width: **To 30 feet**
Color: **Pink, White Flowers; Green, Yellow, Burgundy Foliage**
Bloom Time: **Early Spring**
Special Features: **Fall Color, Attracts Birds, Good for Containers, Slope/Erosion Control**

One of the first trees to flower in spring, redbud is eye candy in every season. Necklaces of tiny flowers garland bare branches in spring. The open, rounded tree canopy provides shade in summer. In fall, the heart-shape leaves turn gold and orange, creating multicolor puddles as they drop. The long, beanlike seedpods persist through the winter. Redbuds thrive in moist soil, especially when young, but will tolerate a variety of soils and drier conditions once established. If you treat your lawn with herbicides, avoid growing a redbud as a lawn tree. Weeping, white-flower, and purple-leaf redbuds are available for special effects.

Plant redbud as a specimen in the landscape, in a group, or in a mixed shrub border. Redbud grows best in full sun or part shade. It does well in the filtered sunlight of woodlandlike situations. It prefers well-drained, moist, deep soil.

A small tree with a spreading, flat-top crown, its trunk often divides close to the ground to give it a broad outline. Transplant container-grown or balled-and-burlapped young trees in spring or fall. Redbuds suffer from drought stress. Water plants deeply during extended dry spells.

Prune plants in spring after they bloom. Canker is the most destructive disease of redbud. It can cause stems to die. Vigorous, healthy plants are rarely affected by canker.

YOU SHOULD KNOW
Although most redbud trees bear pink flowers (hence the name), there are varieties that produce white blooms.

VARIETIES

1. 'FOREST PANSY' offers pink flowers and rich purple foliage in spring that fades to deep green in summer. It grows 30 feet tall and wide. Zones 6–9

2. 'THE RISING SUN' is an exciting dwarf selection that has pink springtime flowers and marmalade-orange new growth that fades to chartreuse before maturing to blue-green. It grows 12 feet tall and wide. Zones 5–9

Saucer Magnolia
Magnolia species

Zones: **4–9**
Light: **Partial Shade, Sun**
Height: **To 30 feet**
Width: **To 30 feet**
Color: **White, Pink, Purple Flowers**
Bloom Time: **Mid- to Late Spring**
Special Features: **Cut Flowers, Fragrant**

Saucer magnolia is a popular small flowering tree that is beloved for reliable blooms. Its 5- to 10-inch-wide white to pink flowers open in mid-spring on leafless branches, and the fragrant flowers last for several days. Dark green leaves follow the flowers and last into fall.

Magnolias thrive in full sun or partial shade. In warm climates, plant them where they will receive a few hours of shade in the heat of the afternoon. They thrive in moist, well-drained soil that is rich in organic matter.

Be sure to site large magnolias where they have plenty of space to expand. Small species can be grown in pots.

Freezing temperatures in spring are most detrimental to magnolias. Even a brief flash of freezing weather will damage or kill fleshy flower buds or newly opened flowers. Protect susceptible plants from spring frost by planting them near a shrub border, hedge, or building that will block chilling winds.

When selecting a species or variety for your region, be mindful of its bloom time. Select a plant that blooms after the last spring frost date for your area.

VARIETIES

1. 'ALEXANDRINA' has flower petals that are dark pink on the outside and white on the inside. Zones 5–9

2. 'NIEMETZI' has a distinct upright form. It grows 20 feet tall and 10 feet wide. Zones 5–9

Serviceberry

Amelanchier

Zones: **2–9**
Light: **Shade, Partial Shade, Sun**
Height: **8–20 feet**
Width: **4–20 feet**
Color: **White Flowers**
Bloom Time: **Spring**
Special Features: **Fall Color, Drought Tolerant, Attracts Birds, Low Maintenance**

Serviceberry is rare in that it offers interest in every season. It kicks off in spring with beautiful white flowers, which develop into tasty red-purple berries that attract birds in early summer. Or harvest the berries and use them to make delicious jams, jellies, and pies. The plant's bright green or bluish-green leaves turn stunning shades of red and orange in fall, and its silvery bark offers winter appeal. Grow serviceberry as a large shrub or small tree. Use this easy-to-grow plant in foundation plantings, mixed shrub borders, and naturalized plantings.

Serviceberry grows well in sun or partial shade. It is a common understory tree in woodlands and tolerates more shade than many other trees. It grows best in moist, well-drained soil but tolerates a wide range of soil conditions. The trees have a small single trunk or multiple stems. It has a broad, flat-top habit. Plant container-grown or balled-and-burlapped plants in spring.

Prune serviceberry in early summer after the plant blooms. This easy-to-grow plant has relatively few pest problems.

YOU SHOULD KNOW
Native to the American Great Plains, serviceberry produces deep purple fruits that make delicious jams, jellies, and pies.

VARIETIES

1. 'AUTUMN BRILLIANCE' is a hybrid with exceptional fall color ranging from orange to red with gold overtones. It grows 15 to 25 feet tall and wide. Zones 4–9

2. AMELANCHIER ARBOREA Common serviceberry is also known as downy serviceberry, which refers to the fine hairs on its leaves and twigs. It grows 15 to 25 feet tall and wide. Its fall color is a delightful mix of orange, red, and gold. Zones 4–9

USDA Plant Hardiness Zone Map

Each plant has an ability to withstand low temperatures. This range of temperatures is expressed as a Zone—and a Zone map shows where you can grow a plant.

Planting for your Zone
The U.S. Department of Agriculture designates 11 Zones from Canada to Mexico, and each represents the lowest expected winter temperature in that area. Each Zone is based on a 10°F difference in minimum temperatures. Once you know your hardiness Zone, you can choose plants for your garden that will flourish. Look for the hardiness Zone on the plant tags of the perennials, trees, and shrubs you buy.

Microclimates in your yard
Not all areas in your yard are the same. Depending on geography, trees, and structures, some spots may receive different sunlight and wind, and consequently experience temperature differences. Take a look around your yard, and you may notice that the same plant comes up sooner in one place than another. This is the microclimate concept in action. A microclimate is an area in your yard that is slightly different (cooler or warmer) than the other areas of your yard.

Create a microclimate
Once you're aware of your yard's microclimates, use them to your advantage. For example, you may be able to grow plants in a sheltered, south-facing garden bed that you can't grow elsewhere in your yard. You can create a microclimate by planting evergreens on the north side of a property to block prevailing winds. Or plant deciduous trees on the south side to provide shade in summer.

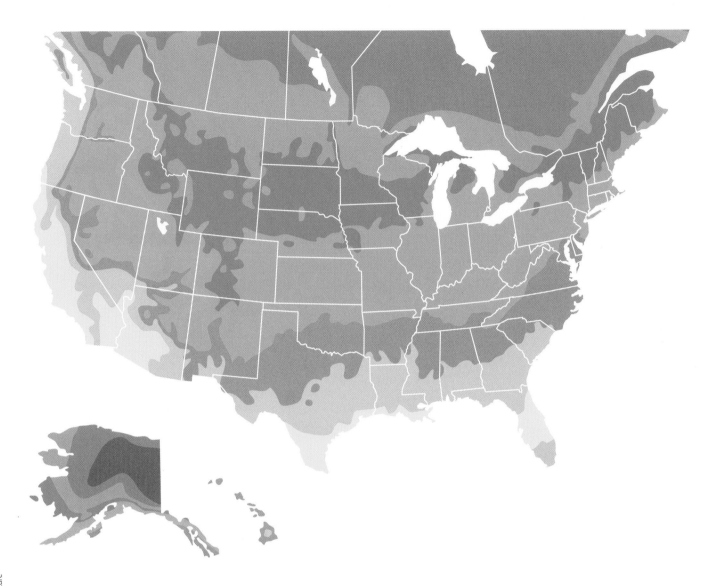

Range of Average Annual Minimum Temperatures for Each Zone

- Zone 1: below -50°F (below -45°C)
- Zone 2: -50 to -40°F (-45 to -40°C)
- Zone 3: -40 to -30°F (-40 to -35°C)
- Zone 4: -30 to -20°F (-35 to -29°C)
- Zone 5: -20 to -10°F (-29 to -23°C)
- Zone 6: -10 to 0°F (-23 to -18°C)
- Zone 7: 0 to 10°F (-18 to -12°C)
- Zone 8: 10 to 20°F (-12 to -7°C)
- Zone 9: 20 to 30°F (-7 to -1°C)
- Zone 10: 30 to 40°F (-1 to 4°C)
- Zone 11: 40°F and above (4°C and above)

opposite Many shade-loving perennials, such as hosta, are widely adaptable to a range of hardiness Zones—from 3 to 9.

Index